THE PROFESSIONAL FE TEACHER

The Professional FE Teacher

Staff development and training
in the corporate college

Edited by
JOCELYN ROBSON
School of Post Compulsory Education and Training
University of Greenwich

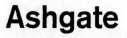

Ashgate

Aldershot • Burlington USA • Singapore • Sydney

Published by
Ashgate Publishing Limited
Gower House
Croft Road
Aldershot
Hants GU11 3HR
England

Ashgate Publishing Company
131 Main Street
Burlington, VT 05401-5600 USA

Ashgate website:http://www.ashgate.com

Reprinted 2000

Typeset by
Kathleen Fedouloff
44 Rosemont Road
London W3 9LY
0181-993 8258

British Library Cataloguing in Publication Data
Professional FE Teacher: Staff Development and
Training in the Corporate College
I. Robson, Jocelyn
374.11460941
ISBN 1 85972 113 3

Library of Congress Catalog Card Number:95-83280

Printed and bound in Great Britain by Biddles Limited,
Guildford and King's Lynn.

Contents

Tables and figures

Contributors

Margaret Adams is Managing Director of The Adams Consultancy Ltd., a business specializing in quality assessment activities. She is a preferred Investors in People consultant with one of the London TECs. She worked as a staff development and quality development practitioner in further education for a number of years.

Bill Bailey holds a Senior Academic post in the School of Post Compulsory Education and Training at the University of Greenwich. He teaches in the area of curriculum and policy developments and has a particular interest in their implications for teachers and managers in post compulsory education and training. He has published articles on the development of secondary and technical education and is a member of the governing body of a further education college.

Derek Betts is Head of Policy at the National Association of Teachers in Further and Higher Education. He has been a full time official of NATFHE for 18 years, concentrating on education policy development since 1984. He is a non-executive director of both BTEC and HEIST. For 12 years, he taught mathematics in secondary schools and in further education.

Michael Bloor teaches education and psychology at the University of Greenwich. He has considerable experience in staff development in post compulsory education and training and has worked in this capacity in the UK, the USA and Australia. His research interests include the accreditation of prior learning and theoretical issues in the acquisition of professional knowledge.

Christine Butterworth teaches education in the School of Post Compulsory Education and Training at the University of Greenwich. She has also worked in the area of staff development for both the Open University and the FEU. She is currently researching the scope and implementation of APL in Higher Education. Her other interests include creative writing and she is the author of several children's books.

Anne Castling is Senior Staff Tutor at Southgate College, and Coordinator of Middlesex University's Certificate in Education (FE). She has worked extensively in staff development in the north east and south east of England, edited the Journal of the National Association for Staff Development and the Journal for Further and Higher Education.

Adrian Chown has taught on a range of AFHE programmes from courses for young adults with Special Needs to post-graduate studies for serving teachers. A Senior Lecturer in Education at Croydon College, he has a professional and research interest in developing practice-based qualifications and training for teachers.

Anne Cox is a Senior Lecturer in the School of Post Compulsory Education and Training at the University of Greenwich. She has been involved in teacher education for a number of years and during 1992/93, she led the syndicate involved in the pilot scheme described in this volume. She has worked as a computer programmer, and taught computer science and Information Technology in Further Education. Her research interests include women and computing and the development of mentoring schemes for student teachers.

John Humphreys qualified initially in Biological Sciences and Oceanography and since then has taught in a number of further education colleges before moving to the University of Greenwich, where he is currently Head of the School of Post Compulsory Education and Training. His current research interest relates to the education and training of Health Care professionals with special reference to funding, education markets and their implications for curriculum design processes. He has also published in the area of science education, where his interests range across ecological education, the learning of scientific concepts and the teaching of evolution and genetics.

John Last was originally a teacher of General Studies. He later became Head of the School of Education and subsequently Assistant Director (HE) at Croydon College. He teaches on their Certificate in Education (FE), B Ed and MA programmes and acts as external examiner for a Certificate in Education (FE) and an MA (FE) scheme.

Jocelyn Robson has a background in film studies, media and communication which she has taught in a number of further and higher education institutions. Currently, she is Subject Leader in the School of Post Compulsory Education and Training at the University of Greenwich. Prior to that, she was Course Director for the full time Certificate in Education course for which the pilot scheme described in this volume was designed. She has published in the areas of gender and film, media education and aspects of the vocational curriculum.

Lorna Unwin is a lecturer in post 16 education and training in the Division of Education at the University of Sheffield, a post she previously held in the Open University's School of Education. As a former teacher in further and adult education, Lorna is particularly interested in ways in which higher education can work more effectively with teachers and support staff in colleges. She also has a research interest in vocational education and workplace learning and has recently completed a study of modern apprenticeships.

Jenny Ware has been teaching for 27 years, mainly in FE. Recently she made a study of literacy/communications teaching in flexible workshops for an M.Phil. thesis for the University of Greenwich. At present, she runs Community Education in an FE college in the Midlands.

Acknowledgements

There are a number of colleagues I wish to thank and they include Professor Maurice Craft, for his encouragement in the early stages of this project, and Gary Culwick for technical advice and assistance. Most of all, I am indebted to my colleague, Bill Bailey, for his unfailing support at all stages of this endeavour.

Thanks are also due to the Journal of Further and Higher Education for permission to reproduce as Chapter 2 the article 'A New Approach to Teacher Training: An Evaluation of a Further and Higher Education Partnership' (from Volume 19, number 2), to the Institution of Mechanical Engineers for permission to reproduce an extract from their Professional Development Record (Chapter 5, Appendix 1), to the Chartered Society of Physiotherapists for permission to reproduce sections of their Professional Development Diary (Chapter 5, Appendix 2) and to the English National Board for Nursing, Midwifery and Health Visiting for permission to reproduce an extract from their Professional Portfolio (Chapter 5, Appendix 3).

Glossary

ABE   Adult Basic Education

ACCESS   An access course prepares mature students without standard (e.g. 'A' level) qualifications to undertake courses of higher education.

AfC   Association for Colleges (which supports and promotes the development of colleges and the sector generally).

ALBSU   Adult Literacy & Basic Skills Unit (government funded organization established in 1980; renamed Basic Skills Agency in 1995).

APEL   Accreditation of Prior Experience and Learning

APL   Accreditation of Prior Learning

BS5750   British Standard for quality management systems in industry. (Renamed ISO9001 in 1994 and now referred to in Britain as BS:EN:ISO9001.)

BTEC   Business & Technology (previously 'Technician') Education Council (awarding and validating body established in 1983 from a merger of BEC and TEC)

C&G   City & Guilds (assessment and awarding body established in 1878).

CATS   Credit Accumulation & Transfer Scheme

CBI	Confederation of British Industry – an employers' organization
CEF	College Employers' Forum
CNAA	Council for National Academic Awards, (validating and awarding body for Higher Education courses in institutions outside the university sector (1964–1992)).
CPD	Continuing Professional Development
CPVE	Certificate in Pre-Vocational Education
DES	Department of Education & Science (replaced in 1992 by DFE)
DFE	Department for Education (replaced in 1995 by Department for Education and Employment).
DHR	Director of Human Resources
ELS	Education Lecturing Services (an organization established in 1995 to provide colleges with part time lecturers).
ENB	English National Board for Nursing, Midwifery and Health Visiting (body which approves institutions offering courses of training for nurses and others at registration and post registration level, e.g. Project 2000).
EO	Equal Opportunities
FE	Further education
FEDA	Further Education Development Agency (which replaced the Further Education Unit and the Further Education Staff College in 1995).
FEFC	Further Education Funding Council (set up in 1992 to allocate finance to the new incorporated FE colleges; two funding councils were set up, one for England and one for Wales).
FEU	Further Education (Curriculum Review & Development) Unit (1976–95)
FTE	Full time Equivalents (students)

GCSE   General Certificate of Secondary Education

GEST   Grants for Education Support and Training (provided by the DES for staff development and training).

GNVQ   General National Vocational Qualification

GRIST   Grant Related In-Service Training (earmarked funds for in-service training for teachers)

GTC   General Teaching Council (proposed body to provide self- regulation of the teaching profession)

HE   Higher education

HMI   Her Majesty's Inspectorate

IiP   Investors in People (national standard for staff development and training, a business-based initiative, managed by the TECs for the Department of Employment).

Industry   Employer-led organizations which define competences for work.
Lead Bodies

Investors in The body responsible for ensuring consistency in the delivery of
People UK   Investors in People on a national basis.

ILEA   Inner London Education Authority (abolished by 1988 Education Act).

ITT   Initial Teacher Training

LEA   Local Education Authority

LEATGS   Local Education Authority Training Grants Scheme

NATFHE   National Association of Teachers in Further and Higher Education

National   The basis of the government's 'standards programme' to develop
Standard(s)   recognized, work-related standards of competence as defined by
              the industry lead bodies.

NJC   National Joint Council (the national negotiating framework for local authority employers and teachers' unions which effectively ceased to operate as far as FEFC colleges were concerned, following incorporation).

NCVQ   National Council for Vocational Qualifications (established in 1986 to rationalize vocational qualifications by creating a framework based on vocational standards of competence required in employment).

NTI   New Training Initiatives (In 1983, a White Paper with this title announced a reform of skills training, adult training and traineeships for 16 year-olds.)

NVQ   National Vocational Qualification (a qualification which meets the requirements of NCVQ).

PROJECT   Name given to the reforms of the initial training of nurses in the
2000   UK which were begun in 1986.

QTS   Qualified Teacher Status

RAC   Regional Advisory Council (a regional body representing the local authority and having responsibility for planning the advanced and non-advanced FE provision in that region. Following the removal of polytechnics and further education colleges from local authority control, the future of the RACs is uncertain.)

Return to   These are access courses.
Learn

SCETT   Standing Committee for the Education and Training of Teachers

SD   Staff development

SLDD   Students with Learning Difficulties and/or Disabilities

STE   Supervised Teaching Experience

TDLB   Training and Development Lead Body (an employer-led body funded by Department for Employment which defines competences/standards for in-company training and development in all sectors of employment).

TEC   Training and Enterprise Council (an employer-led organization whose purpose is to promote and fund training provision in its region).

TRIST   TVEI (q.v.) Related In-Service Training

TTA   Teacher Training Agency (body established in 1994 to fund institutions and accredit courses for teacher training in England and Wales).

TVEI   Technical and Vocational Education Initiative (a programme to introduce vocational studies into schools for 14–18 year-olds, begun in 1983 by the Manpower Services Commission).

VP   Vice Principal (of further education college)

1 Introduction: contextualizing professional development in the new sector

Jocelyn Robson and Bill Bailey

The quality of teaching and learning in the further education sector now matters (and is seen to matter) more than it has ever mattered before. Such are the pressures now on further education colleges that there is a clearly acknowledged need for a more professional approach to staff training and development, for a much wider range of opportunities to meet the diversity of needs in a new time. The Further and Higher Education Act (1992) is, of course, largely responsible for this new emphasis. It has brought about the most significant changes seen in a sector which has been notoriously neglected for decades and it has precipitated some massive shifts in the further education workplace and its culture.

These far-reaching changes and their implications form the context for this book. All the contributors have written in light of their experiences of what these changes mean for the sector. It may be helpful here, therefore, to explain more fully some of the purposes and detail of them.

The 1992 legislation brought about major change in a number of ways. Firstly, further education and sixth form colleges became independent of their local authorities and acquired financial autonomy; they became, like the then polytechnics before them, corporate institutions, with all the legal and financial responsibilities that accompany such status. The Further Education Funding Councils (one for England and one for Wales), which were set up by the Act, have proceeded to allocate resources to the sector using criteria which reflect the government's priorities in relation to training and education for those over the age of 16. These priorities had been clearly identified in the White Paper (1992) 'Education and Training for the 21st Century'; they included a commitment to growth and to a new system of funding which would reward expansion and the achievement of training targets. In addition, some curriculum priorities were identified; in particular, some new qualifications were to be developed as alternatives to 'A' levels.

A consultation document entitled 'Funding Learning' was issued by the Further Education Funding Council (FEFC) in December 1992 and it outlined the funding issues in the sector (FEFC, 1992, a). The situation was complex. The legacy of local authority control was one of considerable variations in levels of funding which reflected LEAs' different priorities and abilities to pay for FE (finance per student ranged from £1485 to £4660 p.a. at the time of incorporation). In turn, this highlighted the need for a funding framework which addressed the government's objectives of increased institutional efficiency and greater student participation. 'Funding Learning' raised these questions and put forward six alternative models for future funding. Colleges were invited to comment on these and, by a large majority, favoured one option (THES, 1993). This 'funding methodology', which is referred to frequently in later chapters of this volume, basically recognized three stages in students' learning programmes: entry, on-programme and achievement. During the later months of 1993, this outline methodology was developed, mainly through the work of the Tariff Advisory Committee which established tariffs (or prices) for different programmes and qualifications. The new system was operational during the college year 1994–95; some small modifications were made to it for 1995–96.

The principal features of the new methodology and their impact on the work and ethos of the colleges are identified in various ways in the chapters that follow. The three elements, or stages, are the points at which resources are released to colleges, on the production of auditable evidence. 'Entry' relates to pre-course guidance and enrolment; 'on-programme' to teaching and tutorial work; 'achievement' relates to the award of a qualification. A further complication is the division of the on-programme phase into three stages; there are three dates on which, to obtain further funding, colleges must provide evidence of students who remain on courses. This is clearly intended to focus the attention of colleges on retaining students and improving pass rates, in contrast with the previous system which simply reflected numbers enrolled in September (Audit Commission/OFSTED, 1993). Other aspects of the methodology, which will not be described here, include 'convergence' to reduce the historical disparities in funding between colleges referred to above and 'clawback', by which colleges repay money to the Funding Council if they fail to achieve the student numbers they have contracted to teach.

The FEFC has also the statutory responsibility of ensuring quality assessment in colleges (FEFC, 1993). The circular 'Assessing Achievement' outlines two means of tackling the quality issue; these are performance indicators and inspection. The first of these requires the college to establish, in consultation with the FEFC, indicators against which its performance will be assessed (e.g. indicators of college effectiveness and of 'value for money' for its students) (FEFC, 1993). It is planned that every four years colleges will be subject to three types of FEFC inspection. Within the four year cycle, there will be inspection by the designated college inspector, by specialist inspectors and finally, by a team of inspectors who will report publicly the information gathered throughout the four year period. Sources of evidence will include direct observation of teaching and training, inspection of students' work and the examination of documentation provided by the college. In the four yearly report, a grade is assigned to each of the following aspects: responsiveness and range of provision; governance and management; students' recruitment, guidance and support; quality assurance; resources (FEFC, 1993). Grades are also given in each curriculum area. The reports on full inspections are published and they are taken into account by the Funding Council when considering future funding. For example, a curriculum area receiving a poor grading at inspection will not receive additional student numbers until it is able to show that it has redressed identified weaknesses.

Under 'quality assurance' is included the college's arrangements for staff development. In their strategic plans for 1994–95, colleges were required to include their proposals for 'planning for quality' and for the development of their 'human resources' (FEFC, 1992, b). This change of terminology in official documentation with regard to planning is indicative of an approach which is more systematic and more related to institutional needs than has been common in the past. Although in its reports on colleges the FEFC inspectorate to date continues to comment on 'staff development', the expectation is nevertheless that human resources development will become more strategic and more directive. Staffing needs will be derived from analyses of the college's objectives and staff development activities will be determined less by perceived individual need than by the college's academic and strategic plans.

These changes are taking place in the context of increased competition for students both between colleges, and between colleges and schools. The intention and the effect of incorporation and the innovations outlined above have been to force colleges to increase levels of participation and to improve quality, in a market situation in which they compete for students. This is clearly in line with government ideology and thinking with regard to all social services and is based on the belief that in the past the FE sector has been less efficient and effective than it could have been in serving public needs – or, to put it another way, the belief that more can be achieved with fewer resources. If expenditure is increased, that is, it can be demonstrated that a corresponding improvement in output (or achievement) has been obtained for the public's investment. To the extent that this greater efficiency is achieved, it is likely that another aim will have been realized – the creation of a new culture and philosophy in FE colleges, as they are required to plan and organize themselves in ways similar to those common in private business and industry. In this context, the adoption of the notion of 'human resource management', as an alternative to staff planning, appraisal and development, has implications for managers of college staff, many of which are explored in later chapters.

3

This, then, is the context in which trainers of FE teachers and staff developers now find themselves working. For the college lecturer, there is an increasing likelihood of bigger classes and a heavier workload. As we have already noted, the quality of the teaching and the learning in FE classrooms now matters more and is likely to be much more closely monitored than in the past. The needs and motivations of FE students are being more carefully considered and institutions are seeking to become more flexible and more business-minded. Staff with college responsibilities often now receive managerial training. The differences between the FE colleges of a decade ago and those of the present are stark.

The contributions to this book reflect this massive shift. Most of the chapters take, as their starting point, a recent experience or innovation in the field of FE training and staff development, reporting directly from those involved, wherever feasible. Thus, the chapters frequently make use of data from interviews, surveys, case studies and evaluations. Overall, a number of key themes emerge. The opinions that the contributors express are, of course, their own and they address the issues in different ways.

As the new corporate FE sector seeks to establish itself, and to come to terms with new constraints, there is an increasing emphasis on professionalism in FE, and a concern with the status of the sector. Existing links with HE institutions are being reworked in a variety of ways; new links are being created.

Collaboration between the further and higher education sectors is the focus of Chapter 2 by Jocelyn Robson and her colleagues which reports on a new partnership scheme in FE teacher training. As noted at the end of that chapter, it is time for all the professionals to be full partners in the initial teacher training process. Otherwise, and especially in view of the setting up of the National Council for Vocational Qualifications, there is a risk of a return to apprenticeship models for all forms of professional training, including teaching.

These concerns, amongst others, underlie Chapter 3 on competence-based teacher training by John Last and Adrian Chown. They describe the emergence of competence-based approaches and their theoretical basis, as well as doubts and concerns about such models. In their analysis of the implications for the profession, they note that FE teachers require coherent initial professional training to graduate level and ask whether the adoption of competence-based qualifications (such as those required by NCVQ) will help us towards that goal.

As the relationship between the HE establishments and their FE partners has changed so, too, has the role of the mentor, conventionally the supervisor of the student teacher's practical classroom experience. In Chapter 4, written by Anne Cox, the role is examined from the perspective of the student teachers themselves. As well as identifying the nature of the support and intervention that student teachers found productive, in terms of their own professional development, this chapter also explains how the process of mentoring can itself be a valuable opportunity for the experienced FE lecturer. Apart from offering a foundation for those wishing to take on staff development roles, mentoring is a

4

useful experience for all FE staff because it involves open discussion and debate about classroom practice and may help prepare colleagues for the more public scrutiny of their work that will follow from inspection and appraisal.

With the growth of the accreditation of prior learning (APL), and of competence-based awards, the production of documentation and evidence, often in the form of a portfolio, is an increasingly familiar strategy on various programmes of professional training and development. Michael Bloor and Christine Butterworth examine the portfolio approach to professional development in Chapter 5. They describe some particular instances of its use, its theoretical underpinnings, as well as some of the issues arising from the practice of, for example, making biographical or personal experience available for assessment and scrutiny by managers and teachers. They also discuss some of the difficulties some students may have, with reflective writing in particular, and they give some guidelines for good practice in the use of portfolios.

As colleges strive to recruit more students and to look for effective ways of retaining them, they are developing strategies to improve student access and to create more flexible modes of student attendance. Chapter 6 on flexible and resource-based learning, written by Jenny Ware, reflects this concern and, as well as describing the nature of the learning that may take place in such environments, she identifies a number of strategies for training staff to work effectively in these more informal settings.

A key role in colleges now is that of the staff development practitioner herself and in Chapter 7, Anne Castling describes how that role has changed with incorporation. As institutions have adopted new management structures, new funding mechanisms, new qualifications, new philosophies and modes of learning as well as new administrative systems, so, too, has the concept of staff development altered. Anne analyses the work of a contemporary staff development team, its relationships and processes and she concludes with an account of the work of two successful staff development networks, involving a number of FE and HE institutions.

Concerns with increased professional accountability in FE have, in part, been responsible for the move by some colleges to adopt quality systems, such as Investors in People (IiP). Chapter 8, by Margaret Adams, examines the processes involved for any college seeking the award and she identifies the benefits available, in staff development terms, from the IiP initiative. Finally, from a number of case studies, she draws out some key issues for both colleges and individuals.

Staff appraisal in FE is the subject of Chapter 9, by Derek Betts. Following the introduction in 1991 of a national appraisal scheme framework for FE staff, subsequent FEFC inspections revealed that staff appraisal schemes were being developed in most colleges. Detailed analysis of the FEFC inspection reports and interviews with FE staff provide the basis for a discussion about the trends that are emerging, of the links with professional development for FE staff and of the future implications for the sector as a whole.

5

As noted, there are now considerable pressures on FE teachers to be more flexible, to achieve more in a shorter time, and the training and development opportunities offered by some distance learning programmes for professionals are of increasing interest to both main grade lecturers and managers in further education. Lorna Unwin, in Chapter 10, describes the challenge for both FE teachers and university lecturers involved in distance learning. In her view, the flexibility and the responsiveness that distance learning can provide should be developed further to facilitate collaborative activity and to encourage FE teachers to see themselves as researchers engaged in critical enquiry.

Overall, the purpose of this book is to encourage good practice in training and staff development for further education, through the dissemination of ideas that work. By critically reflecting on a range of new practices, from both further and higher educational perspectives, the contributors hope to stimulate debate about the future. In the past, the training of teachers for further education and the quality of the teaching experienced by their students have not received the attention they deserve. It is the argument of this book that current changes could (and should) lead to a higher value being placed on the quality of the FE student's learning experience. Certainly, many colleges refer in their strategic plans to their staff being their most important 'resource'. Unfortunately, at present, there is a danger that the contractual dispute and the resource constraints will obscure the benefits available to teachers (and their students) through the adoption of new approaches to professional development. The contributions to this book are evidence of a growing sense of professionalism amongst FE teachers and the chapters suggest various ways in which this professional awareness could be encouraged and developed to the benefit of the sector as a whole.

2 A new approach to teacher training: the further and higher education partnership

Jocelyn Robson, Anne Cox, Bill Bailey and John Humphreys

Introduction

Any form of professional or vocational training (including the training of teachers) can be viewed quite instrumentally in terms of its function of supplying the work force for that profession. Just as in other professions and occupations, there has recently been a concerted attempt to promote and enhance the employer's role, so in education itself, the employers have increasingly become more influential and more involved in the training of their prospective and existing employees.

Conventionally, employers have concerns about their work force which relate both to the number of available employees (from which they will be able to select) and to the quality of the training their prospective employees have received. Methods for ensuring a reasonable match between the demands of employers and the supply (as it were) from the education and training providers are many and various. In the context of education, we see attempts to control the supply of school teachers centrally, in the DFE's allocation of numbers and funds to school teacher training institutions. We are also now seeing attempts in the field of teacher education to control the nature and quality of the training itself, in the proposals to shift those funds away from the HE institutions to the schools (see Education Act, 1993).

Outside education, conventional ways of ensuring employer involvement in the training phase, and therefore of ensuring some restricted employer influence over its quality, have included such strategies as work experience placements and employer advisory groups (both common components of many vocational courses run in the FE sector). Teacher training has, of course, always included work experience and often FE and school staff have been involved as advisors in the planning of the curriculum. Nevertheless, as in other areas of professional and vocational training, there has been a tendency for the educators of teachers

7

to structure and constrain the work experience and to specify the nature and balance of the work that students undertake. Rarely are employers given any direct influence over the operation of the curriculum.

The pre-service training of teachers for further education has escaped the direct official and legislative controls imposed on school teacher education but there have nevertheless been some important shifts of emphasis in this sector, too. Sometimes the reasons for the changes here are similar to those in the maintained school sector but sometimes they are different.

In the maintained school sector, well before DES Circular 9/92 required a greater proportion of school teacher training to take place on school premises (DES, 1992), there had been developments in the delivery of such courses which had affected the balance between the role of the HE institution and that of the school. Both internal and external factors were responsible. Externally, there were a series of measures (e.g. DES, 1984) which sought to shift control away from the HE institutions and which found their final expression in the now abandoned licensed teacher scheme (Wragg, 1990). Internally, within the training institutions themselves, concern to improve the experience of the student teachers had already led, in some cases, to the development of a delivery based on partnership. There were moves to extend the number of days spent in the school, by extending the block placement or, as in the case of the Oxford internship scheme, by arranging for part of every week of the course to be spent in the placement, on a joint or contiguous model (McIntyre, 1990). These changes reportedly brought a greater level of integration between those parts of the course delivered in the HE institution and the school-based experiences; in addition, a closer relationship between the HE and the school staff was developed (McIntyre, 1990).

Wilkin (1990) describes the way in which the curriculum was divided in these partnerships. Following CNAA recommendations (Wharfe and Burrows, 1990), most partnerships stressed a collaborative model in which the school teachers and the HE tutors remained experts in their own areas (Furlong, 1990). These separate roles were seen as complementary but not overlapping in that HE tutors were seen as chiefly concerned with the domain of theory and the school teachers as chiefly concerned with the development and supervision of practice. There has been considerable debate about appropriate areas of responsibility in school-based partnerships and most of it has focused on the need to understand or redefine and work within the framework created by a theory/practice dichotomy (e.g. Alexander, 1990 and Furlong, 1990).

The partnership scheme reported in this chapter, however, can be seen as a more sophisticated attempt to involve education employers and to meet their expectations with regard to the nature and quality of the training given to their prospective staff. Whereas many aspects of our partnership model are not original, we would argue that there are few precedents for the creation of such unified teams of university and employer staff who collectively determine so many aspects of the detailed nature of both the placement and the course experience.

In particular, as will be described later, by operating part of the course on the employers' premises, the scheme enabled FE employers both to contribute to the teaching and, by becoming part of the course team, to contribute to the formulation of plans and schemes of work, formerly the exclusive domain of university staff. There is also the reciprocal effect of linking the university staff to the work placement and its employees in such a way as to require dialogue and to create potentially an effective basis therefore for dismantling the theory/practice dichotomy or ideological mismatches between the placement and the course experiences. Essentially, as will be described, the placement and the course are integrated, not just on the timetable, but also by the overlap of staff who constitute a team. Further, since the model has been designed so that class size corresponds to placement group size, as is explained below, it becomes possible for the first time to build on and extend experiences in all areas, to give employers real opportunities for involvement and influence, and to create genuine opportunities for the development of staff in both sectors.

The time was right, of course, with the increased independence and accountability that had come to the FE sector with incorporation (TES, 1993). Financial pressures and a new competitive status had made FE colleges less willing and to some extent less able to accept student teachers on placement on a goodwill basis alone. Expectations had changed for understandable reasons. Some FE employers clearly felt that they should be recompensed for supervision time and more involved in all aspects of the training of their potential staff; these feelings had to be addressed. Further, the new funding council for the sector was beginning to identify funding criteria, which would specify the need for strategic planning with regard to staff development. As noted elsewhere in this volume, concern over low retention rates in the sector (THES, 1994, a) has created further pressure on college managers to identify ways of enhancing staff performance. The first round of quality inspections by the FEFC reported that almost one in six lessons was of a poor quality and found that procedures for identifying and improving poor teaching were not well developed (THES, 1994, b). In the context of these developments, a scheme which addressed FE employers' concerns about the quality of training available to pre-service teachers was to be immediately welcomed.

There had been some important curriculum developments too, within the sector which influenced the design of our partnership. The awards of the National Council for Vocational Qualifications (NCVQ) brought a stress on the individual achievement of specific itemized competences, as well as an increased emphasis on work-based assessment and successful performance at work, often in highly local contexts (FEU, 1988). Our partnership model effectively acknowledges this greater emphasis on work-based learning and assessment and the increased importance of the employer's role without jeopardizing

9

collective endeavour and peer support and without the loss of opportunities to generalize from specific experiences and to reflect on practice.

Background

During 1992/93, as already indicated, a number of changes were made to the delivery of the full time Cert Ed(FE)/PGCE(FE) course at the University of Greenwich. A scheme was set up to pilot a new way of delivering the course in partnership with four selected FE colleges.

At the time of writing, the full time certificate course is attracting around 380 students each year. It is a one-year course and offers training to people from a wide variety of backgrounds including the sciences, social sciences, humanities, business, technology, tourism, management, marketing, hospitality services, information technology, nursing and so on. The cohort is divided into large groups which are referred to as 'syndicates'. A team of four Greenwich tutors is attached to each syndicate which generally totals around 80 students. Each of the Greenwich tutors has a special responsibility for about 20 students from the syndicate; thus there are four sub-groups, or tutor groups, within each syndicate.

The course is organized into four phases. In the conventional model, students spend the first eight weeks of the course (Phase I) at the University of Greenwich. In Phase II, they begin a two day per week attendance at a placement college, whilst still attending the university for two or three days per week. This contiguous or split attendance pattern runs for seven weeks. Then in Phase III, they begin the block attendance, spending five days per week at their placement college for a period of eight weeks. In the summer term (Phase IV), they return full time to the university.

The pilot scheme involved a variation of the conventional pattern and affected one of the syndicates. Each of the four tutor groups in this syndicate was assigned, along with their tutor from the university, to one of the four FE colleges participating in the scheme. A member of staff from each FE college was identified to act as FE link tutor and partner for the Greenwich tutor.

The students in the pilot syndicate attended their allotted FE college throughout the year. In Phase I, they spent one day a week there; in Phase II, three days a week; in Phase III, five days a week and in Phase IV, one day a week. Over the year, the FE link tutor was involved in the delivery of the course, the organization of mentors and the formal assessment of Supervised Teaching Experience (STE).

The contribution of the FE link tutors to the teaching programme was jointly discussed and agreed according to the requirements of the course and to the individual circumstances and resources of the FE college. It ranged from sessions on classroom interaction, (linked to prearranged classroom observations), the implementation of Equal Opportunities policies in the college, or the role of the FE lecturer, to the setting up and monitoring of curriculum development projects. The joint teaching team of university tutors and FE link tutors for the whole pilot syndicate met together regularly for planning and evaluation and each individual 'pair' of tutors met on a weekly basis at the FE college.

Evaluation

During the year that the pilot scheme was in operation, the views and experiences of those involved were recorded in a number of ways. At the end of Phase I, the students in the pilot syndicate were asked to respond to some open questions about the perceived strengths and weaknesses of both the Greenwich part of the course and the FE college-based part of the course. Later in the year, just before the commencement of their block teaching practice in the FE college, they were given a more detailed and quantitative questionnaire to respond to. Minutes were kept of the meetings between the FE link tutors and the Greenwich tutors, and at the end of the session, all FE link tutors were separately interviewed by the writers. In addition, the four Greenwich tutors for the syndicate were also interviewed. The findings from this evaluation process are reported below.

Induction to the placement
As mentioned, the new mode of delivering the course enabled the student teachers to attend the pilot FE college to which they were attached from the first week of their course to the last. Initially, they were there for just one day each week but by Week 9 this had increased to three days per week and early in the second term, they began their block attendance. Later, during the summer term, the attendance at the FE college returned to the one day per week pattern.

Compared to the conventional model of the course (which had kept students wholly at the university for their first eight weeks and their final term), this changed attendance pattern brought a number of advantages. The student teachers (who were accompanied by their university tutor) had time to establish better relationships with FE staff and to make contacts with the people most likely to be of assistance to them. Appropriate mentors could be allocated much earlier and were then available to assist with the settling in process and with arranging appropriate timetables, tasks that had often previously been left to the student teachers to complete on their own. As a result, student teachers were noticeably more relaxed and more at home in their placements than had often been the case.

They were also noticeably less fearful and anxious about their teaching roles; from the first week of the course, most of them clearly felt as if they belonged, and were members of a profession and a 'culture':

11

I think it made a huge difference. I think contact with the college, knowing the college, contact with the – if you like – significant members of staff in the college... the earlier preparation meant they knew faces, they knew what the college was about, they knew the culture of the college or some aspects of the culture of the college, they... had names, faces to go to... it seemed to me there was a lot less anxiety about that first stage than there has been in previous years. (Interview with link tutor, 1993)

Staff felt that the student teachers gained a better grounding in the workings of the institution and were much more aware of the full range of a lecturer's responsibilities. In addition, it was possible for the FE link tutors to arrange for the student teachers to undertake some direct observation of FE classes much earlier than had previously been possible. In most cases, this occurred during the first few weeks of the course and was an invaluable experience:

I think the early observations are really useful because otherwise what they have in their minds is just fantasy about what goes on. Most of them don't have direct experience of FE, some of them do, but for some of them what goes on in the classroom is just fantasy... it really does help to dispel those... fears and anxieties... about what the (FE) students are like... how easy and difficult it is... is it threatening and so on... and it gives them some idea of what preparation they need to do. (Interview with link tutor, 1993)

Observation of classes in both their specialist and non-specialist subjects gave rise to discussion about the whole range of the FE college's curriculum and provided a great deal of valuable material for later sessions. In addition, the student teachers from the remainder of the syndicate (who were attending different pilot colleges) brought their observation experiences back too, so that overall, tutors felt that an earlier and much better, much richer understanding of the FE college's role and work was achieved.

The FE college involvement
In entering into a formal contract with the university, the four pilot colleges had, in exchange for payment, committed themselves to a partnership for a trial period of two years. That increased commitment was felt on both sides and it gave a new stability to the working relationship and a new impetus to the FE colleges' involvement:

'I think the whole contract has changed the relationship... and the students have a different relationship with the college... in a sense (they) become pseudo-staff much more and there's a much greater

12

responsibility... on standards and ensuring they do well.' (Interview with link tutor, 1993)

The scheme of work to be followed by the syndicate was jointly planned. As mentioned, there were regular meetings at several levels and the FE college inputs were timetabled in consultation with the pilot institutions.

The resources of the whole of the FE institution were now accessible and it was clear that the FE link tutors felt more able to call on their colleagues to support both them and the student teachers from Greenwich. Staff from across the colleges were called in to give specialist inputs, on counselling, careers, equal opportunities, the management of resources and so on.

The university tutors readily acknowledged the worth of the particular contributions that their FE partners had to make in, for example, the setting up of realistic curriculum development projects, in the discussion and analysis of their experience of incorporation, and of the real problems associated with the implementation of policy.

As a result, FE link tutors reported that a great deal of general discussion was generated in the FE colleges by the presence of the student teachers. Later, as mentors were appointed and student teachers moved into classroom roles, there was discussion about what constituted good classroom practice, about teaching strategies, and about what is and is not good professional conduct:

...it has been like a continuous in-service teaching course for a lot of staff; some staff have improved their teaching as a result of working with the student teachers, many of whom were very good... for example, they became more student centred in approach; mentoring forced them to reflect on their own teaching as well as on the student teacher's progress... (Interview with link tutor, 1993)

In other ways too, the Greenwich scheme was seen to have contributed to staff development within the FE institution. Links were made between the requirements of the Greenwich certificate course and those of a college's appraisal scheme, for example, which also included some direct observation of teaching. Another college reported that its own induction provision for new full time staff would have to be enhanced, that there was pressure for it to be at least as good as the programme offered to the student teachers from Greenwich.

From the Greenwich perspective, it was extremely helpful to have a tutor from the university based in the FE college throughout the year. Through dialogue and discussion, through the resolution of particular problems in the day-to-day management of the course and the student teachers, it was felt that a better understanding of the course itself, its aims, its criteria and the concerns of the university to protect the quality of the award was achieved:

13

I must have talked to five members of staff about that student. They were all very worried about it... I was too and they could see I was... the more we talked, the easier it became. It was a problem we could look at together. They could see that I was taking what they said seriously... I explained the procedures we went through in these circumstances and they could see when I turned up with an external examiner... it's not so much a 'them' and 'us' situation. (Interview with Greenwich tutor, 1994)

As the relationship between the partners developed, some issues were raised about their respective roles, especially in the few cases where the student teachers were struggling to meet the demands of the training. Notwithstanding the team approach, at times some differences had to be addressed and they included minor differences in the institutions' disciplinary procedures and codes of practice, for example, as well as more general issues about where overall responsibility for pastoral and academic decisions lay.

Mentoring
As mentioned above, it was possible to identify suitable mentors much earlier in the session and well in advance of any formal assessment taking place. The student teachers clearly benefited as a result and approached assessment with more confidence. Both the FE link tutors and the Greenwich staff noticed an increased level of commitment to the mentor role on the part of the FE staff and in some cases, it was felt that payment to mentors was responsible. In addition, however, the agreement that mentors would take part in the formal assessment of the student teachers in the classroom was perceived as an important shift in policy. Colleges now felt in a stronger position to affect the outcome with regard to particular student teachers and mentors themselves felt they had a fuller role to play and more clearly defined relationships with their mentees.

With a larger number of student teachers present in the college, more FE staff were required to become involved in the mentoring process. This in turn led to discussion and the need for mentors to meet as a group was soon apparent. At meetings with Greenwich staff, and their own colleagues, there were opportunities for mentors to consider, for example, the nature of the monitoring and assessment process they were involved in, to address specific course criteria, to share difficulties and solutions:

We ran several mentor training sessions... covering observation strategy, assessment of teaching... These sessions generated much discussion within the college – for example, what is a good lesson? and so on, and feedback implies it was very good PR for the staff developers and for working with student teachers. (Interview with link tutor, 1993)

14

With the mentors' increased awareness and confidence came, in many cases, stronger, more professional relationships and a collaborative atmosphere in which the student teachers were generally able to relax and grow. University tutors, for their part, felt that responsibility for the training of FE staff was meaningfully shared with the sector for the first time.

Team work

As explained above, each of the four Greenwich tutors in the syndicate was assigned to a pilot FE college and a link person at that college. This paired arrangement worked well on the whole and was supported and monitored by the Syndicate Leader.

Mostly, meetings between the Greenwich tutor and the FE link tutor were scheduled in advance and took place weekly at the FE college. In addition, the Greenwich tutor was timetabled for two hours of tutorial time in the morning of the FE college day and both tutors were timetabled for the two hour taught session in the afternoon. This double staffing allowed the student teachers to experience some continuity and it also meant that the staff were able to support each other as needed. Student teachers quickly became used to seeing the pair as a team:

> The degree of commitment of the college staff and the friendly atmosphere was far above the norm... they were involved and the FE link tutor involved them in such a lot of activities that they were involved both in a timetable sense and in the sense of meeting our students all the time. We were in the staffroom all the time... (Interview with Greenwich tutor, 1994)

As the block approached, Greenwich tutors were encouraged to use some of their contact time for liaising with mentors in the FE college and for supporting them in their assessment role particularly. Throughout the eight week block of teaching practice, the Greenwich tutors were based at the FE colleges and so were also available to their student teachers, not just as occasional visitors, but on a regular basis to advise and support their tutees, as well as to monitor and assess them.

Not surprisingly, some differences emerged amongst the four pilot colleges with regard to details of the implementation of the course and the agreed scheme of work. These differences were discussed at the large team meetings which took place roughly on a termly basis and were usually attended by all the FE link tutors and their four Greenwich partners. These large team meetings were chaired by the Syndicate Leader who, whilst recognizing the need for consistency in order to protect the quality of the award, was also able to negotiate a programme which would allow the FE colleges to make good use of their separate expertise, their particular strengths and their resources in order to help meet the needs of the student teachers.

15

The large team meetings therefore performed an important monitoring function. To some extent, they became the forum for the resolution of difficulties and misunderstandings about the course or about working relationships and they provided a point of reference for tutors away from the individual FE colleges themselves.

Staff from both the FE colleges and the university reported that there was a greater pressure on FE colleagues to resolve difficulties, to work through tricky or demanding situations, to spend more time with struggling student teachers for example, than had previously been the case. Overall, it was felt by staff on both sides that a strong sense of cooperation between institutions developed and that differences were remarkably few.

Peer support
The presence of a whole tutor group (composed of approximately 20 student teachers) in one FE college made a significant impact on the life of that college. There were reservations about the size of this group (especially in the smaller pilot colleges) though it was felt that these concerns had been alleviated to some extent by the change in delivery. As described earlier, this change enabled the FE college to assimilate the student teachers more gradually and gave those student teachers themselves time to become familiar with their surroundings before they embarked on their teaching programmes.

From the student teachers' perspective, the size of their tutorial group and the fact that they were all together in one FE college brought welcome opportunities for peer support and for building a sense of group solidarity. To their Greenwich tutors, (used to travelling far and wide across London and Greater London and even beyond to visit isolated members of the same tutorial group) this was a noticeable improvement. The student teachers actively enjoyed giving and receiving mutual help throughout their block of teaching practice in particular and a healthy, collaborative atmosphere evolved:

> The positive side of the group in the college, even if they didn't get on with everyone in the group... they had people around whose faces they knew and they could see they were going through the same experience and they got a lot of peer support from that... I got the feeling as I went into the college canteen that there would be a group of Greenwich students all sitting around chatting. And if I was going to visit one, they would sit around chatting at the table and say "Whose turn is it today?" and there was a really warm, supportive feel about that... I felt that was a big plus. (Interview with Greenwich tutor, 1994)

> I think it's given them a much more secure base from which to go out and experiment in their teaching. I think they felt much more supported by the group of students and by me... it's given them much

16

more opportunity for reflection and for feeling that they have common problems and they're just much less isolated and the benefits of that are inestimable... (Interview with link tutor, 1993)

There were some cases of isolation due mainly to the existence of split teaching sites and this was reported to have altered the dynamics of the tutorial group in certain ways but even here, there had been opportunities to become acquainted with the environment beforehand. There were informal group meetings at times, arranged by the student teachers themselves (to swap ideas or teaching materials, to discuss difficulties) and the use of the Personal Learning Agenda (a localized Greenwich version of a learning contract or individual action plan) was greatly facilitated. Student teachers (normally in pairs for the PLA) were able to sustain contact throughout the period of the course which they regarded as the most challenging and to continue receiving peer support and guidance with their own learning agendas.

Conclusion

As indicated above, the response to the pilot scheme was overwhelmingly positive. One participating FE tutor described it as 'way off the end of the scale' in terms of providing an improved training experience for the student teachers and the change in the relationship between the FE and HE institutions was also warmly welcomed, especially by university staff.

Through the sharing of both the taught course and the supervision and assessment of practical teaching, FE link tutors were able to contribute to the whole learning experience of the student and an artificial divide between theory and practice was avoided. Several of the FE tutors had already considerable experience as teacher trainers and had taught on their own City and Guilds courses for FE staff. There was never any question that areas of expertise needed separately defining, in the way described by McIntyre, for instance, in his discussion of the Oxford internship scheme:

Fortunately most participants find it rewarding that the expertise they are well placed to provide is valued, and are reassured to know that they need not pretend to kinds of expertise they are not well placed to offer. (McIntyre, 1990, p.114)

This is not to say that our scheme did not allow for the use of institutional and individual expertise but simply that no attempt was made to distinguish between contributions along theory-practice lines. As explained above, both the university tutor and the FE mentor were involved in the formal assessment of practical classroom performance as well as in the delivery of the taught components and the dual perspective thus provided greatly enhanced the students' experience of the course.

Wilkin describes the consequences that follow from a failure to confront the theory/practice dilemma:

> The first of these is that by representing 'theory' as an area of external knowledge, it become possible to exclude it from the training programme. As the importance of practice in school is acknowledged by allocating more student time to it, 'theory' as an item on the timetable can readily be marginalized or even eliminated. Secondly, if practice is viewed as the learning of skills as it is here, rather than as a process of personal and professional development, then there are implied consequences for the assessment of the student. (Wilkin, 1990, p.18)

With the current moves towards competence-based assessment for many professional groups, including teachers, come renewed fears of a return to apprenticeship training, and of the reduction of whole areas of professional knowledge and expertise to sets of demonstrable, itemized competences. The split between theory and practice which is a feature of so many partnerships will do nothing to impede the development of such models and indeed, as Wilkin implies, it may actively facilitate their growth.

Further education, as we are used to claiming, is a very diverse sector with few uniform characteristics. For many, this diversity is its strength and the principal way in which it serves its local populations. In addition to avoiding a damaging theory/practice dichotomy, we were concerned that the design of our partnership should allow for this diversity, that it should prepare student teachers for the richness and the range of the FE sector as a whole.

It was not felt that the FE colleges alone could have provided such diversity of experience or sufficient opportunities for reflection and generalization about experiences. The student teachers themselves were very clear about the value of the university-based part of the course and about the need to have some time away from their placement. For example, it was felt that their first assessment (of a micro teaching session) was best undertaken in the more secure context (as they perceived it) of the university, and that the opportunities of scale offered in the university-based course to join specialist groups (for Special Method or elective courses) enhanced their training considerably. Within the syndicate, grouping and regrouping was possible, especially during the summer term, and this provided further opportunities for student teachers to learn from each other about other FE colleges and about the wealth of variety that exists within the FE sector.

Most FE employers want their employees to be aware of wider perspectives and not trapped at the level of the particular experience. If they are to be innovative and well-informed teachers, they will need to be able to draw on their exposure to a range of involvements and the Greenwich model offers them this opportunity. It has the potential in our view, to lessen the mismatch between FE employers' expectations and the HE training provision, and to increase employer influence over that training, without restricting or jeopardizing the student teacher's opportunities for understanding their experience.

At the 1992 SCETT conference on FE Teacher Education and Training, Peter Chambers called for the establishment of a partnership in the accreditation and delivery of teacher training for FE (Chambers, 1992). He called for a national framework that would formalize the participation of the FE colleges and the training institution in the training programme and declared that the responsibility for developing partnership models now lay with the HE institutions. With the demise of CNAA, the loss of coordinated peer group quality assurance and the fragmentation of FE following the 1992 Further and Higher Education Act, the role of the HE institution has changed; as Chambers stated, HE must now do for its FE partner institutions what CNAA did for them – all the professionals need to be full partners and a concerted effort will be needed to ensure that the training meets employer expectations, encompasses the full range of sophisticated skills that FE teachers need, including those of reflection and evaluation, and remains subject to rigorous validation and professional accrediting criteria.

Though there is no sign as yet of a national framework such as the one proposed by Chambers, the pilot scheme described above does represent, in our view, a progressive response to some of the current concerns of the profession as well as to the political and economic constraints of the times.

Acknowledgements

This chapter could not have been written (nor the pilot scheme itself successfully implemented) without the assistance of Rosie Clark (Westminster College), George Elliott (Richmond Upon Thames Tertiary College), Barry James (Woolwich College), Liz Johnson (Richmond Upon Thames Tertiary College), Pat Randerson (Woolwich College), Joe Watmore (Southwark College), Anne Griffin, Vic Parsons and Keith Wood (University of Greenwich).

3 Competence-based approaches and initial teacher training for FE

John Last and Adrian Chown

Introduction

This chapter examines the provision for initial teacher training in the English further education sector, contrasting earlier courses with those that emerged after the establishment of the National Council for Vocational Qualifications (NCVQ) in 1986 and the consequent development of training courses utilizing competence-based approaches. We consider the strengths and weaknesses of these emerging models and conclude by considering their implications for the future.

Current FE teacher training

A great deal of attention has been focused upon FE following incorporation, associated with its newly identified role in delivering the National Training and Education Targets to improve the vocational qualifications of the work force. So it is worth remembering that during the 1960s and 70s there was also considerable change in the sector, as it adapted to BTEC, CPVE, TVEI and introduced a range of basic skills and Access programmes. However, throughout this time, it received scant attention from the Government or the media, with only the establishment of the Manpower Services Commission in 1973 briefly diverting the educational spotlight away from the school sector.

This may partly explain why the provision of teacher education for FE has lacked the coherence of the school sector, where qualified teacher status (QTS) has long been a necessary entry qualification for the service. Further education, despite its many thousands of students, has had no such common approach to training, and provision has been piecemeal and selective. Research by the Association for Colleges (Gee, 1995) found the number of trained further education teachers in England and Wales in 1991 was only 51% of total staff, rising to 60% with the inclusion of sixth form colleges into the sector. Such a situation is unlikely to continue, as it is likely that funding and inspection bodies, with responsibility for quality audit, will be critical of colleges that do not offer comprehensive staff training for those who enter the profession on the basis of previous vocational or academic achievement but without a teaching qualification. What, then, is the best way forward for FE teacher training?

The provision currently offered in the sector was first considered in the Haycocks Report (1975) which recommended professional training for full and part time staff to Certificate in Education (FE) level and beyond. In addition to some provision offered at regional level by the former Regional Advisory Councils, (mainly focused on staff in adult education), the two main qualifications available to staff are the City and Guilds Teachers Certificate (730), and the Certificate in Education (FE). The 730 is offered by FE Colleges, and the Certificate is offered by colleges in partnership with universities or by universities alone, either as a one year full time or a two year part time course.

However, whilst the attendance mode, content and curriculum model of these courses is not uniform, experience of validation and external examination by the Council for National Academic Awards (CNAA) and moderation by City and Guilds shows that they share common philosophical approaches. These can be characterized by commitment to:
• developing the autonomy of adult learners
• the use of the learning group of trainee teachers as a resource
• negotiation of content, providing a flexible curriculum model which developed and adapted as the FE sector itself changed
• the sharing of teaching input between teaching staff and the learning group
• the continuing education of teachers, as education professionals working within a broader social context.

Such provision stressed the role of critical self-reflection as a key aspect of the learning process, drawing on the work of Kolb and Fry (1975), Usher (1985), and the concept of the reflective practitioner (Schon, 1983). On this point, Her Majesty's Inspectorate (HMI), in their survey of Certificate of Education (FE) courses, note that two of the most positive features were the valuable resource created when groups of individuals with a wide experience of the sector study together, and the use made of this by tutors to support the development of reflective practice (HMI, 1992). As Ashworth (1992) notes, collaboration and teamwork are key components of being competent as a teacher.

HMI and CNAA reports provide evidence that the Certificate of Education (FE) had a curriculum model which reflected best practice in the sector, so that it was – and is – largely successful in both its professional training and general educational aims. It is an acknowledged higher education award and, as such, offers a progression route into degrees and postgraduate study. We would not, of course, wish to describe this provision, based as it is on the humanist learning tradition, as some kind of educational arcadia! However, whatever its flaws, it

21

has acknowledged strengths and newly emerging provision must be evaluated in comparison to it.

The emergence of competence-based models

With the establishment of the NCVQ, English education experienced its first introduction to a competence-based curriculum model which emerged in the USA in the 1950s and 60s. Given the time of its development, it is probably unsurprising that it is based on a philosophy that is, as Tuxworth (1986) notes 'unashamedly behaviourist' in character, drawing heavily upon the process of functional analysis to identify job competencies. This places it in the tradition of behavioural psychologists, such as Skinner, and theorists of behavioural objectives, such as Bloom (1956). Without commenting at this point upon the desirability of such an approach, it was clear that there would be tension between these programmes and existing FE teacher training. However, given that the Certificate in Education (FE) has adapted to reflect new curriculum models within the sector, it was equally inevitable that competence-based provision for FE staff would be developed! We now consider the case made to support these emerging models and analyse their impact.

One of the first papers to offer a positive response to a competence-based curriculum was from the Further Education Unit (FEU) in 'Towards a Competence-Based System' (1984), although it should be acknowledged that their concept of competence laid greater stress on the role of knowledge than did the subsequent NCVQ model.

This paper supports a concept of education and training based upon 'competence rather than time-serving' and goes on to define a competence-based approach as one with:

- a careful definition of the competence to be mastered (to include sufficient skills, knowledge, appropriate attitudes and experience for successful performance in life roles)
- an understanding of the definition (of the task to be performed) by the learner
- an acknowledgement of the wide range of ways through which learners acquire competence (to include a wider definition of learning than solely classroom-based activity, with specific recognition of learning in the workplace)
- valid assessment and accreditation procedures.

These precepts, and the basic NCVQ structure of units, elements and performance criteria, began to be incorporated into a number of FE teacher training courses. In 1989, the University of Ulster instituted such a scheme as 'a recognition of the important changes taking place' in further education, arguing that 'a sensible way to introduce students to competence-based education... was to let them experience [it] themselves'. (Stark and McAleavy, 1992, p.81) Similar schemes were introduced by several colleges and universities while the City and Guilds, (as part of an Institute policy to move to NCVQ programmes), introduced competence-based versions of their 730 Teachers' Certificate (the 7305 and 7306).

At the same time a variety of industry 'lead bodies' emerged which, using design criteria devised by the NCVQ, produced generic standards to identify and describe a minimum level of competent practice in an occupational area. No education lead body was established, but early in 1991, the Training and Development Lead Body (TDLB) produced competencies for national standards in commercial training (not education). Following a pilot study, the FEU proposed that an amended form of these standards should be used as the basis for FE staff training.

Advantages of the competence-based model

During these developments a number of benefits have come to be associated with competence – based qualifications and training (UDACE, 1989). The most general claim is that the provision empowers learners, with programmes based not on attendance, but on the needs and skills of individuals. The programmes are also associated with an acknowledgement that learners have an entitlement to clear statements of:
- what it is intended people will know and be able to do as a result of successfully completing the programme
- what they will need to demonstrate they know and can do to be assessed as proficient
- the criteria against which their knowledge and abilities will be assessed
- the ways and contexts in which knowledge and abilities can be demonstrated, together with a recognition that the widest possible range of appropriate ways and contexts will be accepted
- a recognition that prior learning, both formal and experiential, will be acknowledged and accredited.

Associated benefits in the way provision is organized include:
- open learning with flexible patterns of attendance, modes of study and a wide range of resource-based learning
- distance and extra mural learning in a variety of contexts, including home and place of work
- programmes divided into units or modules which enable the learners to deal with them in an order and time span appropriate to their own needs
- unified structures of equivalence and progression which provide compatible certificates of Credit Accumulation and Transfer Schemes (CATS).

Furthermore, the development of the TDLB standards, and their significant championing by FEU and adoption within the 730 by City and Guilds, led to other claims in support of the model, including:

- the benefit of a national framework of accreditation based on national competence-based standards
- clear rates of progression, based on CATS for progression through teacher training into management qualifications
- national standards to provide a nationally consistent means of describing the professionalism of staff. (FEU, 1992, p.1–2)

Finally, there has developed a body of evaluative material based upon the experience of FE staff as learners on competence-based training programmes which supports several of the points above. One such study (Stark and McAleavy, 1992) is typical in citing as benefits:

- the clear identification of the tasks to be undertaken in order to achieve success
- an open and identifiable system of assessment
- the ability to receive credit for previously acquired skills and knowledge
- improved motivation, based upon the above.

Such findings also reflect the experience of staff involved in the delivery of NVQs in general, for example in Business Studies and Hairdressing (Raggatt, 1994), and there is little doubt that the NCVQ programme of far-reaching and fundamental changes has had a major impact upon both FE and FE teacher training.

Two cheers for competence?

Some of the benefits identified above clearly improve on the position of FE teacher training prior to 1986 – especially the concept of a clear and unified framework for professional training and subsequent continuous professional development – so why only grudging praise for competence?

Principally, it is because most of the features listed and regarded as benefits are not *necessarily* related to the model and not one is *exclusive* to competence-based curricula. We can take two often quoted benefits as examples. The accreditation of previously acquired learning, both formal and experiential, can be given against any programme with clear outcomes and assessment criteria, while modular frameworks are commonplace without competence-based curricula. Similarly, whilst applauding openness in assessment criteria, we must also ask if the standards are really 'nationally consistent' and better than previous models?

As we have described, prior to the introduction of competence-based programmes, FE teacher training had a model which placed the learner, and the process of learning, at the centre of the curriculum, while concepts like autonomy, negotiation and group learning as well as critical reflection and personal development were inherent in the principles of FE teacher training and

FE provision, (witness, for example, the development of Access courses). In general terms 'the competence revolution' has served to highlight several desirable features for education programmes. However the key questions must be whether a competence approach can:

- improve on previous provision in enabling FE staff to understand the learning process, such that they can, in turn, help their own students to learn and develop;
- deliver better quality training, and hence produce better staff for the FE sector.

We remain unconvinced of their ability to do this; our reasons will be discussed in the following sections.

Current approaches to competence: the doubts and concerns

1   Objections to the behaviourist psychological principles
As stated earlier, the current national design criteria for competence-based qual-ifications are based on behaviourist psychological principles. These principles are controversial, and there are ethical and practical reasons for questioning the wisdom of adopting them for education generally, and for teacher education in particular (Bull, 1985; Hyland, 1994; Smithers, 1994).

Principally, there is the objection that a behaviourist functional analysis of work roles produces profiles of competence which reduce complex practice to a series of discrete, mechanical acts and confine the goals of learning to what can be most easily prescribed, measured and observed (Ashworth and Saxton, 1990; Marshall, 1991; Hyland, 1993). These limitations lie behind the most common and fundamental objection to a behaviourist model of competence for teacher education: that it provides a limited and fragmentary conception of the teacher's role (Tuxworth, 1982; Chown and Last, 1994). A particular concern is that this approach has difficulty in describing how teachers manage the rapidly changing and unpredictable circumstances of individual learning, and in accounting for the role of knowledge in practice.

2   A limited view of what it means to be competent.
The concept of competence which underpins a competence-based approach to teacher education is plainly of crucial importance. Only when we have a clear and adequate definition of what competence refers to can we begin to identify and describe what competent practice as a teacher entails.

Curiously, the NCVQ *'Criteria and guidance'* notes do not offer a definition of competence, but they do define an element of competence as: 'a description of an action, behaviour or outcome which [a] person should be able to demon-strate and [which] should be a single function attributable to an individual'. (NCVQ, 1995, p.24) Logically then, competence in the NCVQ model seems

25

no more than the ability to perform all the prescribed behavioural actions identified as elements in a functional analysis of occupational roles. However, the NCVQ (1995) also uses the term 'competence' at various times to refer to:

- the application of knowledge, understanding, theory, principles and cognitive skills
- planning and problem solving
- dealing with contingent circumstances
- working with people
- creativity
- ethics and values
- and transferring competence to new situations.

This list of characteristics sits uneasily with the underpinning behaviourist concept of competence, and it suggests that within the current NCVQ model competence has, at best, an 'unclear logical status'. (Ashworth, 1990, p.9)

While some of these characteristics may be susceptible to a prescriptive functional analysis, it is doubtful whether others are. It is particularly difficult, for example, to see how we could prescribe the behavioural outcomes which must occur when people act creatively, solve genuine problems, make ethical or value judgements and cope with the unexpected or unpredictable. Yet teachers, in our experience, are frequently called upon to act in just these pragmatic ways to support and promote the learning of the individuals they teach, and effective pragmatism – incorporating reflective practice – seems an essential attribute of practice as a teacher.

The NCVQ acknowledges that profiles of competence should include attributes like these. The general descriptions for NVQ levels 3, 4 and 5 refer to the exercise of 'personal autonomy' in competent practice, while at Level 5 competence is said to involve 'the application of a significant range of fundamental principles and complex techniques across a wide and often unpredictable range of contexts'. (NCVQ, 1995, p.11) But the question at issue is whether the NCVQ's current approach can adequately acknowledge and account for all these characteristics when it lacks an adequate, clear and logically consistent concept of competence (Hodkinson, 1992) and, therefore, whether this approach offers an improvement on the other models of initial teacher training described above.

There is little evidence that lead body standards devised according to current NCVQ design criteria can adequately reflect these capabilities, perhaps because the criteria themselves are muddled. They appear to assume that people behave pragmatically by adapting their behaviour; however, this assumption is logically inconsistent with the behaviourist principle of training individuals to respond in a uniform, predictable manner to predetermined situations (Ramsay, 1993). As a result, the current approach to competence seems unable to offer an account of how teachers autonomously adapt their practice, or of the knowledge and thought which informs this process.

3   The role of knowledge and thought in practice

The NCVQ acknowledges that 'effective performance depends on the individual having an appropriate body of knowledge, theory, principles and cognitive skills on which to draw' because 'performance and knowledge are intertwined in competence'. (NCVQ, 1995, pp.17, 30) But they offer no account of the *kinds* of complex cognition that professional practice might entail; nor do they offer an explanation of how performance, knowledge and thought are '*intertwined'* in practice. As a result, there is a tendency in standards to reduce cognition to knowledge, and knowledge to the demonstrable possession of factual information (Norris, 1991). This tendency gives rise to a worrying separation of performance and cognition, with the latter in some unspecified subsidiary or 'supporting role'. When this is combined with an assumption that both cognition and performance can be easily disaggregated and atomized into elements which neatly and conveniently cross-match, the result is that 'the role of knowledge is reduced to tiny bits corresponding to the performance criteria'. (Smithers, 1994, p.14–15)

Despite some attempts by the NCVQ to address these concerns, for example in the design of GNVQs, it is difficult to see how the current approach can avoid this failing so long as it insists on the essential premise that complex practice can be reduced to itemized lists of observable behaviour (or the outcomes of behaviour) which can be 'objectively' prescribed and measured. This forces NVQ profiles of competence to focus on what people can 'show they know' at the moment of assessment, rather than trying to uncover the complex cognitive resources which generate the integrated process of their practice over time.

4   The 'deskilling' of practice.

A particular concern for people who are involved in initial teacher training and staff development is that the limitations in the design of current competence-based qualifications have the potential to 'deskill' professional practice. Competent practice is presented in the current approach as a series of static and discrete elements, combined rather arbitrarily into units. Individual units are said to have 'coherence', but they are not seen as linked together in any larger, necessarily coherent process. The NCVQ (1995) insists that each unit of competence must be available for separate assessment and accreditation, and that units can be achieved in any order, with few time constraints. Therefore, it is quite possible, for example, to deal with a unit on assessment before one on diagnosing and establishing learning needs and goals. Once each unit of competence has been demonstrated and accredited, it can be ignored while another is pursued.

There may be a certain logic in adopting this approach for the accreditation of prior experiential learning. But it seems wholly inappropriate as a basis for systematic professional training, because it has the potential to deprive training for practice of coherence and integration. As Smithers points out, is 'there is no guarantee that aggregating numerous individual "competencies" will amount to a skilled overall performance... it is how they are put together that matters'. (Smithers, 1995, p.11) The NCVQ model, however, has difficulty in acknowledging any sense of sequence or interrelationship because the principles on which it is based drive it in the opposite direction, towards disaggregation and reductive analysis. This incomplete, 'piecemeal' approach misrepresents the complex nature of what Ryle (1949) calls 'intelligent practice' (Hodkinson, 1992). It provides an account of practice and a basis for assessment which are both inadequate, with a consequent potential deskilling effect.

Callender (1992) cites evidence of employers who support staff in training only for those NVQ units which are of immediate benefit to the employer. A particular concern in education is that untrained, or partly trained staff will be encouraged to take on new duties and responsibilities without proper preparation, and then undergo APEL to 'qualify' after the event. This type of policy would clearly raise important issues of quality, and equality of access to fully trained, professionally skilled teachers.

A second concern stems from the prescriptive and directive nature of the NCVQ design criteria. One declared aim behind the introduction of NVQs is to shift control of the design of work-related qualifications from universities and colleges to employers through the introduction of lead bodies. However, while lead bodies are indeed responsible for devising and maintaining the national standards for their occupations, in practice control has been brought back to the centre, to the government. Each lead body must have Department of Employment recognition; the department determines the structure of each lead body and the lead bodies draw up standards according to the design criteria issued by the NCVQ (NCVQ, 1995). Thus, while qualifications for FE teacher education were previously devised by practitioners and their university colleagues, in the future they will be centrally determined by means of 'desk research'. (FEU, 1995, p.7)

At the time of writing (April 1995), there is no lead body for education. However, an examination of the TDLB Standards suggests that when the current prescriptive approach is applied to teaching, it reduces the autonomy of both teachers and learners, and redefines the nature of professional practice. In particular, it neglects the need for teachers to develop a critically evaluative aspect to practice – at an individual, organizational and national level. Ecclestone, for example, argues that with the introduction of NVQs learning has become 'tied to increasingly centralized definitions of outcome', with 'personal needs and ambitions for learning... explicitly wedded to the needs of the economy'. (Ecclestone, 1993, p.13) One consequence of these 'detailed and prescriptive specifications' is 'teachers increasingly becoming technicians, administering other people's definitions of outcome'. What is lost, Ecclestone points out, is 'education to challenge, disagree and change society; questions about morals, ethics and professional values'. (Ecclestone, 1993, p.12)

In a similar vein, Hyland suggests that the NCVQ approach is 'likely to produce teachers who are "competent" yet largely ignorant of the wider cultural, social and political context in which the role of the teacher needs to be located' (Hyland, 1993, p.18). Such teachers, he fears, will be neither experts nor reflective practitioners.

The problems in assessment

1   The over specification of routine tasks
In principle, the NCVQ's determination to secure a nationally valid and reliable system of criterion-referenced assessment for vocational qualifications has its merits. However, Wolf argues that, no matter how detailed they are, assessment specifications cannot 'carry unambiguously all the information required about the domains or outcomes in question'. 'Perfect transparency is not to be had,' she claims, 'and searching for it merely produces a forest of verbiage' (Wolf, 1993, p.10). There is a concern that the NCVQ has been tempted by what Wolf calls the 'seductive promise of complete clarity', with two damaging consequences. First, the design criteria have produced 'a never ending spiral of specification' (Wolf, 1993, p.15). Second, in the current approach, each routine task is analysed microscopically while, as we have seen in previous sections, what is non-routine, complex or difficult to describe is ignored or glossed over (Tuxworth, 1989).

2   A misrepresentation of the assessment process
Currently, the NCVQ insists that a candidate's performance must be assessed against each and every element, performance criterion and range statement (NCVQ, 1995). But many are concerned that this misrepresents the real nature of both human performance and assessment (Wolf, 1993; FEU, 1994). In practice, reliable assessment is said to be a complex process which ultimately relies on the skilled judgements of experts using holistic models of performance. These expert judgements have a 'compensatory' aspect in which the lapses and strengths in a person's performance are offset against one another to produce a realistic assessment of their working practice (Wolf, 1993; FEU, 1994). The current approach to the assessment of competence precludes such judgements, insisting instead that hundreds of immensely detailed, discrete assessment criteria must each be equally applied.

3   'Endless recording of achievement at the cost of learning'
Teachers commonly express two particular complaints about the practical consequences of this approach (FEU, 1994). The first is that the current NCVQ design criteria lead to a lack of coherence in the learning experience and assessment programme (FEU, 1994). Teachers on our Certificate in Education

programmes, for example, often refer to the development of a 'tick-box' mentality in which their students become obsessed with being accredited for individual elements. And our own experience of delivering the City and Guilds 7305 Teacher's Certificate showed us that when teachers participate as learners in this kind of approach, despite the best efforts of the tutors, they all too easily develop the same mentality. This inherent tendency to focus on discrete 'items' of performance makes it difficult to develop a sense of learning and practice as a complex, integrated and dynamic process.

The second complaint is that the assessment process comes to dominate education and training, entailing 'endless recording of achievement at the cost of learning'. (FEU, 1994, p.9) In short, 'the assessment tail has come to wag the learning dog'.

The result is that the current competence-based approach gives misleading messages about learning and assessment. Ecclestone, for example, argues that teachers are 'led to believe that knowledge only exists to underpin performance' and there is 'a growing tendency to dismiss anything which is not assessed' (Ecclestone, 1995, p.9). Consequently, teachers and learners adopt a strategy of 'teaching and learning to the test'.

4   A minimal threshold and binary judgements

In the NCVQ competence model, assessment decisions are based on 'a threshold standard which seeks only to distinguish competent from not yet competent'. (UDACE, 1989, p.31) When a person provides evidence of their ability to perform all the functions of a job role set out in the competence profile, they are deemed to have crossed the threshold and to be competent. Assessors can therefore only make a simple 'binary' judgement about the quality of a person's performance; it is either 'not competent' or it is 'competent'.

This has two disturbing consequences. First, the profile of competence provided by the standards is never more than a profile of *minimal* competence; it identifies the minimum acceptable level of autonomous practice expected in the occupation (NCVQ, 1995).

Second, if, after someone has been deemed 'competent', the quality of their performance improves – if they become more competent at their job – the current NCVQ model cannot acknowledge this. It only recognizes a change in competence when a person changes the functional role they perform within an organization – in other words, when their job changes.

Because of those limitations, the NCVQ model cannot identify or recognize a development in the quality of practice beyond the level of minimal competence to the level of, say, being proficient or expert. It is difficult, therefore, to see how the NCVQ competence-based approach can assist us if we want to devise or accredit programmes which are intended to encourage people to develop their professional practice beyond the level of the minimal threshold towards excellence.

30

The way ahead?

The current approach to competence begins from two simple proposals: firstly, that occupational qualifications and training should be based on profiles of occupational practice and that assessment should focus on evidence of capability to practise; secondly, that all occupational qualifications should be part of an integrated system.

Whilst there are potential benefits in this approach, its success clearly depends on our ability to model and assess practice in an adequate and effective manner.

The NCVQ has insisted that all work roles – from shelf stacking to brain surgery – can be profiled and assessed using a single, ubiquitous method of functional analysis based on behaviourist psychological principles. However, as we have pointed out, there is continuing doubt about the suitability of this approach for the initial training and continuing development of teachers.[1]

In 1991, the FEU suggested the amended form of the TDLB standards be adopted for qualifications and training in the FE sector, a proposal which remains controversial. In a further development, the Further Education Development Agency (FEDA) assumed responsibility in April 1995 for managing, on behalf of the Department of Employment, the production of an 'occupational and functional map of the FE sector'. The intention, as this book goes to press, is to produce an account of jobs, roles and responsibilities within the sector which is 'complete, relevant and credible', and the project report is expected to be used to inform the decisions of Government ministers 'on the way ahead' (FEU, 1995, p.7).

There are three questions which we hope the project will answer.

1 If we accept the initial proposals of the current approach, does it necessarily follow that the same method of analysis is appropriate for all kinds of complex occupational practice? Might there be other methods which are better able to describe what teachers do and know? (Chown, 1994; Winter, 1992).[2]

2 The current approach substitutes for universities' and colleges' curricula (which can be adapted in response to local and national developments) a centrally produced set of national standards, which cannot be devised or altered rapidly. How will this improve on previous teacher training provision and its capacity to develop autonomous reflective practitioners who are flexible and responsive to change in 'classes' and their workplace?

3 Existing Certificate in Education (FE) programmes provide personal and professional development to the level of first year degree study. In our view, teachers who are able to respond effectively to the needs of adult learners in a rapidly changing FE sector require coherent initial professional training to graduate level. Will the adoption of competence-based qualifications in the NCVQ mould help us towards the ambition? Will they at least maintain the

31

current position? Or will they have the effect of removing FE teacher training from HE altogether, with a consequent loss of professionalism to the detriment of the sector?

The answers to these questions are awaited with interest.

Notes

1   A similar concern has been expressed by Peter Smith over the introduction of NVQs into architecture (Times Higher Educational Supplement, 24 February 1995, p.12)
2   In this context, it is interesting to note that the problem of representing the complexity of what professionals do in their work has been addressed by Gonczi and colleagues in Australia who are attempting to avoid the fracture between skills and knowledge (Gonczi, 1994).

4 Teacher as mentor: opportunities for professional development

Anne Cox

Introduction

This chapter sets out to explore the role of the mentor in further education colleges from the perspective of the student teacher. In particular, it examines the aspects of the role in terms of intervention and support that the student teachers found productive. It draws out from this some pointers for the development of both beginning and experienced lecturers, and links this with the need for the more open discussion of classroom performance.

Role of the mentor

The role of the mentor in education has been the focus of some attention in recent years. The shift towards partnership in the training of school teachers has led to a change in the role of the staff who support the student teacher during the placement in school, and there has been extensive discussion of this (see for example, Wilkin, 1990). Similarly, there has a move to involve further education colleges more in the training of staff for the post compulsory sector (see for example the discussion of the University of Greenwich partnership in Chapter 2). As the relationship between the HE establishments and their FE partners has changed, so too have the roles of the mentors in the colleges.

Additionally, changes in funding arrangements for colleges have affected the work of the lecturer. As discussed in Chapter 1, high levels of student retention are now rewarded and so greater emphasis is now placed on lecturers' pastoral roles. This has clear implications for staff development. Since mentoring involves tutoring and counselling student teachers, the lessons learnt from it will be useful in many contexts.

Although many accounts of mentoring are written from the mentors' perspective (see for example, McIntyre and Haggar, 1993; Williams, 1993), some work has been done to examine the needs of the student teachers themselves in schools. Furlong (1990) has examined student teachers' views of their training in the context of partnership. Booth (1993), concentrating on the mentoring of student teachers, has given an account of supervision during block teaching practice. In this study, student teachers were asked to describe the process of being mentored and to evaluate it: they looked for positive, unthreatening, readily available support, and practical advice on subject specific teaching and classroom management. Tickle (1993), also taking the mentoring relationship as his focus, examined the 'effectiveness' of exchanges between mentor and mentee from the perspective of the student teachers. In his account, he describes how the student teachers relied 'on their individual world of ideas, thoughts and emotions... in effect they were engaged in a self reliant, analytical and technical concern with what worked in practice... there was little opportunity or desire for public debate' (Tickle, 1993, p 204).

Following an approach similar to that of Booth and Tickle, this chapter takes as its starting point the accounts of three beginning lecturers in further education, who were asked to look back on their time as student teachers, and reflect on their experience of being mentored.

Context

The three lecturers – P, N and T – whose accounts are given here, had been full time students on the Greenwich PGCE(FE)/Certificate in Education (FE) course. All three had been placed in the same further education college for Supervised Teaching Experience (STE). This college is one of the partner colleges which works with the university in the partnership scheme. Under this arrangement, students attend both the university and the further education college throughout the year. Each student teacher is allocated a mentor in the further education college, who is involved in teaching in the same subject area as the student teacher. This mentor is responsible for supervising the student teacher on a day-to-day basis during the block placement of STE. Most mentors are selected from experienced staff; usually they are main grade lecturers at the top of the scale; occasionally they are senior lecturers. A mentor contract (which is a form of learning contract, in which both mentor and student teacher are asked to identify their expectations of each other during STE) was adopted. This contract was signed by both mentor and student teacher, and both kept copies.

34

P, N and T were interviewed during the spring term in the academic year following their completion of the Greenwich PGCE(FE)/Certificate in Education (FE) course. All three, by this time, were working as visiting lecturers in the further education college where they had been placed for Supervised Teaching Experience. The timing of the interviews allowed all three to evaluate, reasonably objectively, the contributions that their relationships with their mentors had made, yet the experience was recent enough to remain fresh in their memories. These three are case studies from which general points may be drawn; they are not a random sample.

During the interviews, the three lecturers, P, N and T, were invited to look back on their periods of STE and to describe the aspects of the mentor/student teacher relationship that had been helpful. They were also asked to describe what they imagined to be an 'ideal' mentor. They had had contrasting experiences. Both P and N felt that they had had positive experiences of being mentored. T had had a less satisfactory relationship with her mentor, but had had excellent supervision from another member of staff whose class she had taught, and who had supported her informally.

P's story [1]

P had had a mentor she had found to be very effective; her mentor had acted as a 'sounding board' for ideas and P stressed how comfortable and safe their working relationship had been:

> I had a very good mentoring experience. I was able to approach my mentor and ask him questions without feeling a fool, without feeling inhibited. The most important thing was not feeling a fool for asking. He made me want to become better – he encouraged me to try things – [he said] 'go on and do it!' Other mentors seemed to hold people back. He gave me the freedom to choose; for example, whether or not I wanted him to remain in the first lesson with me... That was amazing... to build up confidence without some one watching me... [My] mentor gave me ideas: we talked about diagrams... about recent developments in [our subject], ... before the class so I knew the timings, [and] the scheme of work. I had the material – he was always giving me things. We did a joint tutorial together, and that was a very good experience. I'd never done anything jointly with a teacher before so it was like observation as well as teaching... [I would have] found it pretty uncomfortable to discuss colleagues' practices and give my own personal opinions. When you are a student you have to try to be as discreet as possible.

The majority of teachers have developed their own techniques through years of experience [and their] experience [is] taken for granted.

Here, P identifies some of the key aspects of her view of effective mentoring. Most importantly, she feels that it is essential that the student teacher feels psychologically safe in the relationship with the mentor, that the mentor is sympathetic, reassuring and encouraging. However, she thinks that it was important for the mentor to go beyond this, to stimulate the student teacher to improve. She also found significant the mentor's roles as advisor, as a provider of teaching materials and as a fellow subject specialist with whom she could discuss developments in her subject area. P found that discussing the performances of her mentor's colleagues was not easy, and she had not been able to use her mentor to help her reflect critically on her observations of other teachers.

Crucially, there is the suggestion that decisions about how the mentoring and supervision would be implemented were taken jointly. Her mentor had given her the freedom to make decisions about his role; for example, she was consulted about the timing and frequency of his classroom observations. Working together in a team-teaching situation seems to have strengthened the sharing of responsibility in the relationship.

P observes that the mentor's own confidence as a lecturer was important: 'my style of teaching is slightly different from his and of course the students noticed it and compared. They always do – somebody else could feel threatened'. P says her mentor was an ideal mentor: 'I wouldn't change a thing'.

N's story
Like P, N described her mentor in positive terms; she stressed the importance of relationships and spoke appreciatively of her mentor in this context:

Everybody here was really friendly – I find that helpful, really did... I was welcomed in the college. [There was a] good atmosphere. Teachers are frantically busy – running around. You know you're being a nuisance if you ask things, but if people's approach is warm and welcoming, that really made me feel great. Lots of changes going on here, people are really tied up, and people have got their own agendas as well. I did feel [my mentor] pushed me in at the deep end – that's quite realistic actually, but actually she was monitoring what I was doing. I realised that she was doing it very discreetly... She didn't give me *too* much support – she knew when to be there when not to be there. I needed the experience of getting on with it really, and knowing I could do it gave me some self confidence. We had a regular session and that was helpful, [when] I got stuck with a new group [or] materials and she made helpful suggestions...

The importance of being welcomed echoes P's comments about feeling accepted. Like P, N feels that the relationship is one in which she can express herself safely. Like P, N also identifies the need to strike a balance between close support and the freedom to try things out for herself. However, N's mentor seems to have been unsure of the feedback N would have liked; unlike P's interaction with her mentor, there seems to have been no discussion at an early stage about the negotiable parts of the mentor role. For example, there were some problems concerning the feedback on lessons that had been informally observed:

> She sat in some of my sessions. I think I would have liked her to say 'that went OK', and she didn't, unless I asked. That's OK – you have a feeling about some classes, but others you're not so sure. I had a query about whether I was explaining what I wanted students to do clearly enough – you know I felt I hadn't done that – maybe it could have been a bit more forthcoming. Some people think if you don't actually ask for it you don't want it, they feel awkward about giving you feedback. I could have done with a bit more really. When I was [formally] assessed that was absolutely thorough and helpful... she picked up points I hadn't thought about at all, which was helpful... I probably hadn't made it clear in the contract in the beginning, that that's what I wanted to do, in fact I wasn't clear myself at the time. I'm clearer now.

> [An ideal mentor would] give *lots* of feedback every session... not watch *everything* that would be intimidating but... a balance. The student (who's already feeling observed anyway) [mustn't be] under a microscope – that would be awful, that would be *really* inhibiting, I think. I think it's just getting the balance really; plenty of feedback but not overdoing it...; not to be slow at giving feedback, to be quite reassuring . Because I didn't ask for feedback quite a lot of the time... in the first couple of weeks... unsure... later you can judge for yourself. But when you first do it, you've no idea, you've no benchmark, [you] don't know what... you know it in theory, you've seen other people, your own practice... Maybe look at lesson plans beforehand: not all of them; but ones that – some seemed quite straightforward and I had a good idea straight away and they fell into place – others I struggled with gauging how much to cover. In the first week, you do need to be a bit more spoon-fed, then eased off quickly after that. I do think it is important to let people get on with it: you have to do that in the real world.

Now, as a visiting lecturer in her first year of teaching, N's priorities are with the subject content of her lessons:

I am more concerned about content so I don't always pay as much attention to teaching strategies as I should do. Really it's easy to get into one way and then you get [too] bogged down... [I need] to think about that.

N's account shows that the needs of the student teacher change with time. The mentor needs to be quite directive at the start of STE, but the student teacher needs space and autonomy to develop, and to take increased responsibility for the lessons as the block progresses. The decision about which particular issues the mentor needs to look at with the student teacher must be shared. For example, N needed to agree with her mentor which particular lesson plans needed to be looked at together. In her account of the ideal mentor, N gives the impression of searching, as she talks, to clarify retrospectively her own needs. She seems to be exploring, perhaps for the first time, how she and her mentor could have worked on this together. Although the relationship seems to have been supportive and effective, there seems to have been little of the discussion of what was required by the student teacher that P describes, and fewer opportunities to negotiate.

T's story
At the time of the interview, T , like P and N, was employed at the college where she had done her Supervised Teaching Experience. Here, she describes her mentor:

I would have liked more time with my mentor – she said at the beginning 'just do the... unit – do it whatever way you want.' So she gave me a lot of scope; but I think when you're starting I think you need more boundaries, and more – you know – something to hang on to... [to know] what I *need* to do, (not that I wanted to do exactly what anyone else was doing) but I needed to know what they were doing so that... base my decision on what I would do... It's just that feeling that you're out there swimming by yourself; you're not quite sure if this is right or not right.

One thing [my mentor] said, 'I should have looked at your plans more – I should have looked at what you were doing'; and at the very beginning I would have liked that. I mean it would have been helpful the first couple of sessions to look at my plan and see... I think it was all right for me, because I *do* like to just do things my own way as long as I've got that underlying support. But then I think talking to other people – I don't think *they* would have enjoyed that: they needed more support... maybe the mentors need *more* discussion with the university... how to do observation and give feedback... some of the [mentor's] comments... I thought, 'why are you saying that?' ...I didn't think that was a helpful comment to make.

38

Although T does not want to be 'spoon-fed', she wants the opportunity to talk through plans and ideas. She wants the freedom to experiment within boundaries – to find her own style. Her mentor has not provided her with enough opportunities before a class to discuss plans together, or after a class to describe, analyse and reflect on her teaching – T would have welcomed more opportunities for dialogue with her mentor. In contrast, T enjoyed working with another lecturer, G. T taught G's GCSE group during Supervised Teaching Experience. They shared the teaching by splitting the afternoon session: T taught the first half until break, G the second. This is T's account of how they planned the teaching and discussed the classes afterwards:

> The thing that G did with me with the GCSE classes... she told me what topic I was going to cover and they had a particular book they were using. So I went through it all, [to] do all my preparation, and then I'd go in and have lunch with her just before the class and she'd talk through everything just to make sure that I had all the points that needed to be covered... That was helpful. She also had GCSE questions, so... she did most of the sample essays. But sometimes I did that as well... the actual topic then reinforced with the questions.
>
> [Interviewer: Did she watch you teach?] No she left me on my own with that... [that] was fine. I think she checked with the students afterwards; she said she'd got some very good feedback... I'd discuss [the lesson] afterwards. I'd go and have a cup of tea afterwards at tea break time... if I hadn't covered everything I'd planned, she'd just – she's amazing, she'd just go in there without any notes at all and talk the hind legs off a donkey! I felt very confident with that way of working. How I actually put it over was entirely up to me, ...she just wanted... to give me the support, to say, this is what we need you to cover and how you do that is up to you. Because my style is very different to hers: she did a lot of talking, and I gradually... more interaction with the students got them talking a bit more...

Together, T and G established a way of working that suited both of them. T was given a well defined framework in terms of content within which she felt free to experiment. G provided safety in a number of ways: she accepted T's performance without being too judgemental, and she provided a safety net in practical terms – she was flexible enough to correct any of T's errors or to compensate for any omissions on T's part. T felt safe and had a partner for regular discussion. Like P, she was participating in a form of collaborative or team teaching; also like P, she felt that the fact that her style of teaching provided a vivid

39

contrast to that of her collaborator. This contrast in teaching styles may have helped them establish productive relationships with their mentors.

Discussion: the process of effective mentoring

A number of points emerge from listening to the student teachers' stories. All three mention – either directly or obliquely – the importance of feeling psychologically safe in the relationship with their mentors. It is important that the mentors are non-judgemental and accept and support the student teachers' views and efforts. This safety allows mentors to find the right balance between directing the student teachers and giving them the freedom to experiment, to find their own ways of teaching. The mentor, ideally, suggests ideas to support the student teachers in planning the lesson, describes how the topic is often taught, provides ideas for assessment strategies, materials, and resources. However, the student teachers need to feel free to decide on the details of the plan within this framework.

The mentor's own confidence in his or her own teaching style is an important factor. This contributes to the safety of the relationship and to the mentor's ability to support reflection. The mentor needs to feel unthreatened by the student teacher, and to be open enough about his or her own practice to appreciate a choice of strategy which does not necessarily replicate the mentor's own style. A contrast between the mentor and the student teacher helps the mentor's ability to support the student: both P and T, in the interviews, comment on the positive effects of the difference between their mentor's teaching style and their own.

The support required varies with time and the relationship between mentor and student teacher needs to be periodically renegotiated. In the cases where the working relationship is an effective one, and the student teacher and the mentor spend productive time together on a regular basis, this will emerge naturally. However, where there is uncertainty about the expectations of the relationship on either side, or there is insecurity, or there is not enough time to discuss the development of the student teacher's requirements, there is a danger that the relationship will remain fixed at the level of the initial needs of the student teacher, or, in some cases (as with T's mentor) the mentor will simply retreat.

Problems emerge, too, when, the supervisor's responsibilities are not clear to either the mentor or the student teacher. For example, the role of the mentor in observation of the student's classroom performance and the subsequent debriefing caused both N and T and their mentors some problems. Although the student teachers all welcomed the opportunity to teach unobserved, informal feedback, as N points out, is important in the early stages, particularly when the student teachers feel unable to judge their own performance. In T's case, her mentor's debriefing skills needed development. Both N and T refer to the monitoring of their performance using student feedback to the class teacher or the mentor. Neither student teacher expressed negative feelings about this as a procedure, but this course of action is not explained by the mentor, or agreed with the student teacher, and the criteria by which such additional feedback is judged are not explicit. Such opaque procedures could leave less confident or less successful student teachers feeling vulnerable.

Taking time to discuss these processes is essential. Although P and T said that they would have liked to have spent more time with their mentors, they acknowledge that mentors are 'busy, busy people'. It is essential, therefore, that the time spent mentoring is managed efficiently, and that the needs and expectations on both sides are made explicit. Wherever possible, the procedures used for mentoring should be examined, should be agreed between the mentor and the student teacher, and be revised regularly.

In order to be an effective mentor, the skills of effective tutoring are required. These skills enable mentors to provide a safe learning environment for the student teachers which encourages them to experiment freely within safe bounds. These skills also enable mentors to encourage the critical and constructive discussion of lesson planning and classroom performance. Effective mentors should be confident enough in their own teaching ability to accept and foster, where appropriate, a student teacher's alternative approach. Crucially, the mentors need to be able to help the student teacher to reflect critically on their own practice and to be able to engage in the dialogue which makes good practice explicit.

In addition, although the mentor contract was designed to facilitate the establishment of a safe relationship, it was not used as effectively as it might have been. The contract should enable the mentor and the mentee to use their time together productively. It should also allow them to make agendas on both sides clearer, to address the power imbalance in the relationship and to adapt their relationship to changing circumstances. The contract should be seen as the basis of a flexible arrangement which allows for renegotiation and clarification; it should not be seen as a fixed agreement which effectively constrains both parties.

Conclusion

There is an absence, in further education, of a culture which encourages or even allows open discussion of teaching. In order to have effective mentoring, the mentor and the student teacher must step outside the normal conventions of staffroom discourse and openly discuss, evaluate and reflect on practice. This can be very difficult for both parties. P remarked that she was 'pretty uncomfortable' about discussing colleagues' practice; although this is said from the perspective of a student teacher, it is likely that many further education lecturers would feel the same about the open discussion of colleagues' work. Expecting the mentor and student teacher to engage in regular reflective dialogue about

41

pedagogy is therefore demanding a great deal. There are, however, other models of mentoring such as peer or collaborative mentoring, where colleagues can provide support for each other (see McCann and Radford, 1990). In this context, the imbalance of power is less of an issue and the tension generated by the assessment function of the mentor is absent. The discussion of one's own and a collaborating colleague's teaching can be developed in a supportive atmosphere, in a constructive, private dialogue.

Here, the lessons from the experiences of the student teachers described above are valuable. Lecturers need to be able to look at their own teaching critically, in an atmosphere of mutual support and psychological safety similar to that which good mentors create for their student teachers. By learning from the experience of being a mentor, lecturers not only learn about their ability as mentors but they develop valuable skills for peer support, too.

However, the privacy of this exchange is a limitation. In order for individuals to benefit more completely from talking about their teaching and listening to each other, there needs to be a shift from the private dialogue to more open discussion in colleges. Tickle (1993) describes the need to develop this culture of open discussion. Without it, he argues, learning about teaching might be dominated by the narrow source of knowledge rooted in personal, private experience; open debate is necessary for the full development of the reflective practitioner and for professional growth.

Recent changes have created pressure to encourage this open debate. The introduction of appraisals (discussed in Chapter 9), which may include the observation of classroom performance, means that classroom teaching is a less private activity than it has been in the past. Experienced lecturers' performance is now discussed in a dialogue as part of staff development. In some staff development schemes, this is linked to college-wide evaluation. Even more publicly, the reports from college inspections, which include assessment of the quality of teaching performance, are generally available. Wider discussion of teaching, both in private dialogue and in college-wide debate, will help prepare lecturers for these exercises and will support their further professional development in the colleges.

Finally, mentoring offers a valuable opportunity for the lecturer who is interested in moving towards a career of managing staff development. The traditional way to promotion has begun with course leadership and those who are interested in the professional development of staff have usually transferred from managing student learning to managing staff development. Mentoring offers an alternative to this. It gives lecturers an opportunity early in their careers to take responsibility for supervising the development of others' pedagogic skills. This is a sound foundation for those who wish to take on college-wide staff management and development roles in the future.

Acting as a mentor, therefore, can be an important opportunity for a lecturer. The experience can inform the mentor's practice outside their interactions with student teachers. Now that the critical observation of teaching is both more important and more public than it has been before, it is in the best interests of lecturers to take on board the lessons learnt from listening to student teachers' descriptions of effective mentoring.

Note

1   The interviews were recorded and transcribed. In the extracts included here, ... indicates omissions from the quotation; [ ] indicates insertions for clarity; *italicised* words indicate emphasis.

Acknowledgement

The mentor contract was originally developed with Batch Hales of The Education Centre, Wellington, New Zealand.

5 The portfolio approach to professional development

Michael Bloor and Christine Butterworth

Introduction

Many programmes of professional development in the field of post compulsory education and training now require participants to complete a cumulative documentary record of their experiences. These records may be called logs, diaries, or portfolios. They complement formally assessed course work or tests, and may contribute to final assessment.

The spread of portfolios has been fairly recent and rapid and not much is yet known about how they are used: formal evaluation of their design and application has been slow to be disseminated. This is partly because the single term 'portfolio' refers to many different kinds of document. The portfolio compiler may be an employee planning their career route through a company, a student writing a record of their time on a training course, or an applicant to a college or university putting together a claim for the accreditation of prior learning.

Some common generic purposes can be identified across this range of examples, however. This chapter looks at various examples of portfolios currently in use to identify these common purposes. We will elaborate the learning theory on which portfolios are based, and describe elements of good practice in their use. Finally, we raise some general issues related to the use of portfolios in the current context of professional development and training.

Portfolios and their purposes

Portfolios and professionalism
Traditionally in fields of education such as art and architecture, a portfolio was a collection of samples of a student's work, demonstrating the range of their achievements and illustrating the level of their abilities. Why should a way of

44

demonstrating creative achievement have spread so rapidly into other professional fields?

Handy (1990) relates portfolios to changes in professional careers. He describes the decline of the 'traditional' professional pattern of long term, specialized employment, and the rise of the multiskilled professional working for many employers on a consultancy or short term contract basis. Handy advocates the portfolio (which he describes as '…a collection of different items, but a collection which has a theme to it' Handy, 1990, p.146) as a way of giving coherence to the complexity and variety of such a professional work record.

The portfolio as a record of experience
This is the first common purpose that different types of portfolio share: they are a record of the individual's work tasks and training. One institution advocating the use of portfolios as a 'portable record' of professional experience is the Institution of Mechanical Engineers. Under its Monitored Professional Development Scheme, engineers working towards chartered status keep a record showing how their training and work experience are meeting the Institute's standards. Graduate engineers, for example in the Ford Motor Company, work with a mentor to draw up an individual training plan that will help them achieve the defined objectives required for Chartered status. They then record their progress towards these goals.

The portfolio as a guide in career planning
Such a training plan is an example of the second common feature of the portfolio as a vehicle for professional development. The portfolio is not only product (a work record), it is also part of the process of career planning. It can be used to help the individual plan their progress towards further levels of professional expertise. Once they have achieved Chartered Status, engineers can use the Institution's Professional Development Record to plan their continuing professional development. An extract from the Institution's leaflet on this career planning portfolio is in Appendix 1.

At BP, employees are offered Personal Development Planning as a process that will support self-assessment, goal identification and career planning. In a computer-based scheme, the employee can identify and review their own interests, values and abilities and relate these to their career options to help them plan their development within the organization. The scheme is optional, and can be linked to appraisal if the employee wishes.

These two purposes – recording experience and planning career development – are consistent with Handy's definition of a portfolio. The Institution of Mechanical Engineers Monitored Professional Development Scheme requires something additional, however. The individual is expected to write up a critique of their experience at regular intervals. This critical and evaluative purpose links this industrial example with portfolio developments in fields such as nursing and teaching, where one influential model of practice predominates: the reflective professional.

The portfolio as a support for critical reflection and the application of theory
Handy and other writers on the structure of work (Schon, 1991, Ch. 1) emphasize the pace of change and the growing complexity of professional roles. This need for flexibility, together with an interest in accountability and effectiveness has led to the redefinition of the model of professional expertise. Recent work (e.g. Schon (op. cit. and 1987), Kolb (1984), and Boud et al. (1985)) has identified the process of critical introspection (or reflection) as a necessary stage in their model of professional learning. This developmental model of experiential learning has been very influential in fields such as nursing and teaching. The model stresses two aims: firstly, the usefulness of articulating the personal meaning of an experience (reflection), and secondly, the linking of knowledge to its practical application (conceptualization and critical evaluation). These are the final two common purposes of many portfolios: to support reflexivity and to connect theory with practice. Compiling a portfolio is an opportunity for the individual to undertake regular periods of reflection on their experience. Articulating these reflections in written accounts helps the development of self awareness. On formal programmes of training and development, the trainee or student can use the formal theory they encounter in the taught course to help them analyse incidents at work.

The next section will look in detail at examples of portfolios currently used on programmes of initial professional training and in-service professional development in the fields of health and education. The description will cover the contents and structure of the portfolios, and give details of the support provided during the compilation.

Examples of portfolios used in teacher training and professional development at the University of Greenwich

Portfolios on initial training courses at Greenwich The part time Certificate in Education requires students to complete a reflective practitioner portfolio (for each of the two levels of the programme), rated at 15 credit points (the value of a unit within the credit accumulation scheme). The structure is provided by the specified learning outcomes for the portfolio unit itself. These relate to various aspects of their professional work both inside and outside the classroom, and tutors' observations of their teaching. They are also asked to evaluate their own professional development during their time on the programme. Written work for each outcome must link to unit content where appropriate. In this portfolio, there are not separate sections or pages for the recording and reflective purposes: each entry combines the two. Three different preprinted sheets are provided as models that students can use for

46

their entry. They can use these to write up a critical incident, a diary entry, or a book review.

The full time pre-service Certificate in Education (FE) /PGCE(FE) course requires students to compile a portfolio during their Supervised Teaching Experience (STE) or placement. This STE log or portfolio contains all of the documentation relevant to the achievement of the Supervised Teaching Experience unit goals, such as evaluations of the student's own and observed teaching, lesson plans and formal teaching assessment reports. This STE portfolio therefore provides a record of experience, a means of identifying professional development and also encourages reflection. Linking theory and practice is achieved by a subsequent unit – Learning from Experience. This is a synoptic unit requiring reflection upon the STE portfolio, identification of further professional development issues, and illumination of these issues by production of an assignment which incorporates relevant educational theory and literature.

The professional development portfolio on the BA (Education and Training) This in-service BA at the University of Greenwich for practitioners in the field of post-compulsory education requires all students to complete a portfolio during their time on the programme. Completion of the portfolio is rated at 15 credit points and it is graded on the quality of reflection demonstrated in the cumulative entries, to enable the grade to count towards the final degree classification. The BA is a longer and more elaborate programme than the initial training Certificate, and professionals who take it are usually mid-career. Consequently the portfolio is a more complex document, with separate sections covering all four portfolio purposes.

In one section, the student logs their work experience, filing details of work tasks, in-service courses attended, etc. Other sections fulfil the reflective and critically evaluative purpose: there are weekly sheets on which they are encouraged to note their reading, and relate theoretical ideas met in the taught units to their experiences at work. At the end of each semester (also the end of the unit) the student teacher records their overall reflection on the professional value of their study. This semesterly entry is used during a formative assessment tutorial, and it is intended to aid cohesion in a unitized, part time programme. These in-service portfolios also ask the student teachers to document their development on the programme, something which is felt to be desirable in a modularized curriculum.

Portfolios for health professionals
The Greenwich examples above all operate inside particular programmes. Health professionals such as nurses and physiotherapists are two occupational groups who may accumulate their professional development via short, often uncertificated courses taken in various training and work organizations. Their own professional bodies have each produced a central version of a portfolio for individuals to use.

The professional development diary for physiotherapists Updating and extending the professional expertise of physiotherapists has until recently been up to individuals or their employers, who may be hospitals, GP practices, or occupational health centres in businesses: others are self-employed in their own practices. The Chartered Society is putting in place a national system of professional qualifications, working with various universities. (The BSc Hons in Physiotherapy Studies and the planned MSc in Reflective Practice at the University of Greenwich are two examples.)

The Society's strategy is to develop a professional culture which accepts continuing education and development as part of a physiotherapist's working life. The Professional Development Diary is part of this strategy. It has been introduced into Schools of Physiotherapy as part of initial training, and is available on request to qualified practitioners. Since it is aimed at practitioners in initial training and those in mid-career, the diary is a fairly complex document. It fulfils all four core portfolio purposes, each of which has a separate section. (See Appendix 2 for an extract defining its purpose and structure.) Each section has preprinted formats to help structure the entry.

The diary has been designed to be used as a distance learning device. This, together with the variety of its users, means that many sections contain substantial additional material explaining the concept of the reflective professional and its underpinning model of experiential learning. There is also self-assessment material to help the physiotherapist identify their learning style, and examples of completed entries. In effect, this diary has a fifth purpose: that of educating the individual using it about its philosophy and methodology.

The ENB professional portfolio With the onset of Project 2000, nursing has begun the process of becoming a graduate profession. As with physiotherapy, the strategy of the professional body is to raise the qualification level of the occupational group, and stress is laid on the process of professional development. A qualifications' framework has been developed to rationalise and add coherence to the range of post qualification training courses available to nurses and other health professionals.

The ENB Professional Portfolio is provided for qualified practitioners to help them plan and record their progress through the framework. (For a summary of the Portfolio's aims, see Appendix 3.) There are preprinted sections for recording and evaluating formal and informal training and work experiences. Entries for these sections can include the identification of achievements which may be used to claim accreditation of prior learning. The purpose of supporting reflective practice is achieved in a section allowing for critical reflection on particular, significant incidents.

Nurses keeping the Professional Portfolio can also use it to help their progress on a particular qualification: the ENB Higher Award. This award requires demonstrated achievement in ten areas of professional expertise, and one

48

section of the portfolio is structured to aid action planning to achieve learning in these areas. Like the physiotherapists' diary, the ENB portfolio is a complex document with sections for each of what we have distinguished as the core portfolio purposes. Both portfolios also share an educative purpose: to define and explain the concept of the reflective practitioner in order to help with portfolio completion. These portfolios are being used as a device to disseminate this concept at an important stage in the professionalization of both these occupational groups.

Core purposes of the portfolios
The above examples of portfolios currently in use in training and development show a high degree of overlap. Each one shows some selection of at least one of the four core purposes:
* recording training and work experience
* planning professional and career development
* supporting critical reflection
* linking theory and practice.

The particular emphasis on a purpose may vary because of the context in which it is used: course-based or work-based. We can call these the explicit purposes, since they are stated in each portfolio. The educative purpose, central to the last two examples, is a more implicit purpose insofar as it is contributing to a changing professional culture. It is important for their professional socialization that these portfolio users understand and learn to behave in accordance with this model of professional expertise. In the next section, we examine the theoretical principles underlying the portfolio development process.

The theory of learning underlying portfolios

The portfolio as a model of experiential learning and reflection.
Drawing upon models of experiential learning that emphasize the importance of reflection (Kolb, 1984; Boud et al., 1985; Gibbs 1988) a model of the portfolio process can be developed.

The portfolio can be seen as a systematic documentation of each of these four stages of experiential learning:

Stage 1   Experience.
Stage 2   Recall of relevant experiences and reflective observation on these.
Stage 3   Drawing conclusions; this involves some personal analysis and interpretation by the candidate. As we have already seen, some portfolio formats require the candidate to go beyond this and incorporate some critical analysis which may be informed by reference to current research and theories in their professional area.

49

Stage 4   Application of conclusions and implications for future professional development.

This stage requires the candidate to indicate how the processes of documenting experience, reflection and analysis will inform, enhance and illuminate their future professional practice.

The function which the portfolio is serving, however, and to some extent, the professional context in which it is being used will determine the emphasis placed on each of the stages. For example, those concerned with documenting and evidencing learning for career development (e.g. the Institution of Mechanical Engineers' example) will focus mainly on stage 1, using the portfolio as a recording device. Those emphasizing the development of professional reflection will focus more on stages 2–4.

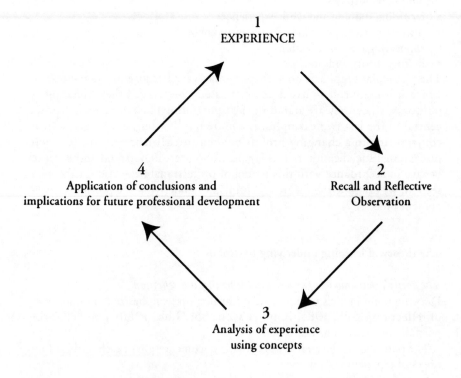

Figure 5.1 A model of portfolio processes

Role of formal and informal theory in portfolio-based learning
Informal evaluation at Greenwich has shown that one of the areas of difficulty in portfolio work is that of incorporating formal theory into reflective writing. Since Schon (1991), learning theorists have written extensively about the

distinctive characteristics of experiential learning and there is much current controversy about the role that formal theory should play in such accounts. Usher (in Bright, 1989) distinguishes practitioner, or informal theory, that is created through experience in a particular work context, from formal theory, which is the sort of knowledge and understanding which is usually taught formally on academic and professional courses. Informal theory, Usher argues, is created through practice and is the result of the interaction between the practitioner's experience and the cognitive models s/he uses to structure the interpretation of their experience. The argument is that practitioner theory is legitimate and deserves the status of a discourse in its own right. However, the problem with informal or practitioner theory is that it is privately experienced, frequently intuitive and therefore not known, and is dependent on the context in which it was generated. Jarvis (1994) also points out that it may be essentially conservative and inflexible unless interrupted or challenged by critical incidents which demand reassessment.

One purpose of some portfolios is to provide an opportunity through the reflective accounts for candidates to make their informal theory more explicit. Through reflection, this informal or practitioner theory can be made more thematic and more explicit. This results in what Argyris and Schon (1980) refer to as 'espoused theory'. Candidates need to provide a reflective, articulated account of their practitioner theory in order to generate their espoused theory: this is not an easy task. There are ways of facilitating the documentation of espoused theory. Writing in the first person does in some ways support this process. This can enhance the sense of personal ownership and is consistent with the personal nature of practitioner theory. Portfolio counsellors can also facilitate this process by supporting and providing feedback to the candidate (Bloor and Butterworth, 1994).

When portfolios are assessed for academic credit, critical evaluation of identified practitioner theory using formal theory may be an important requirement. The idea is to encourage the candidate to use formal theory from relevant professional research and literature to review, evaluate and reconsider their practice. This should necessarily involve some elaboration and reorganization of the person's existing constructions of informal theory.

Case study
The following case study from a portfolio submitted for the purpose of accreditation of prior experience and learning (APEL) on the University of Greenwich BA (Education and Training) course is a useful illustration.

The candidate was describing his experiences of education management during a period of institutional amalgamation:

> During the development of the first matrix structure, I was a member of the Academic Board as a staff representative. I spoke in favour of the

initial proposals to go matrix as a result of my observations concerning the disadvantages of the previous, traditional structure which had become bureaucratic and non-reactive to changes in demand. Reflecting upon the situation at the time, I believed that the majority of the proponents for change were of this opinion not because of the advantages offered by the matrix concept but because we simply felt a change was needed. At the time, many colleges were flirting with the concepts involved and some had already taken the plunge but we did not model our structure upon them. There was a lack of understanding as to what 'matrix' meant let alone how it could be applied to a specialist college such as ours.

Perhaps if we had considered Scott (1981) when he described the matrix as a 'high demand and high stress situation' the concept would not have been so appealing. However, he also outlines the advantages of the system as being a way of achieving greater flexibility, improving reaction to external forces and providing the personnel with greater challenges. The first two points were obviously going to be needed at this juncture as we had just joined another Institution and the final point was wanted by many staff.

At the time we did not use Knight's (1977) models but simply relied upon what we regarded as being basic management theory. It is possible to analyse retrospectively our decisions by adopting his approach and this reflection has led me to believe that an error was made in the selection of the wrong type of matrix structure.

In this example, the APEL counsellor had made some suggestions for further reading in the area of education management and the student had selected from this and produced this account. The extract demonstrates the use of formal theory to review, develop and refine informal practitioner theory. Although this function of portfolios is a most productive one, it is, as already indicated, not an easy process for the candidate. Indeed, the portfolios that do emphasize this purpose, (e.g. the Greenwich BA, the ENB and Physiotherapy portfolios) all now provide extra material to help candidates with the process, as a result of feedback about difficulties experienced.

The biographical approach
Recent research on teacher thinking and teacher socialization acknowledges the importance of biographical experience in both the professional socialization of teachers and upon their informal theories about education (e.g. Butt, 1984). The argument is that it is not so much the formal career of teachers that is crucial, but the developments in professional life, as experienced by the teachers

themselves, because these help form a sense of professional self and a framework of informal educational theory (Kelchtermans, 1994).

This approach shares distinct links with earlier work done by psychologists working in a tradition of humanistic or perceptual psychology. For example, Combs and Soper (1963) examined the differences between 'good' and 'poor' professional helpers. They investigated counsellors, members of the clergy, and social workers and teachers, and concluded that becoming a good member of these helping professions is not just a matter of acquiring appropriate skills and expertise, but was also a question of personal discovery, of learning how to use oneself well. They called this the 'self-as-instrument' concept. The biographical approach argues that by writing a professional biography, the candidate will make their own subjective informal theory explicit and more coherent in the reconstruction. One example of this rationale is provided by Calderhead and James (1992) who explore how a portfolio (in the form of a record of experience on teaching practice) can be used to help students appreciate the impact of their own biography upon their teaching.

There is also a current interest in social research in how autobiographical narrative can demonstrate the dialectical relationship between the subjective meanings in the narrative and the social context in which it was produced. Portfolios such as those described in this chapter are examples of a group of 'administrative innovations' similar to the extended CVs analysed by Miller and Morgan (1993). Such innovations are institutional requirements that individuals produce 'thematic' or rational biographical narratives that are goal directed and produced according to guidelines. Miller and Morgan point out, however, that even explicit guidelines cannot cover everything: the writer still needs a tacit understanding of institutional expectations to help select relevant material and present it in the appropriate way. Trying to satisfy these expectations increases the difficulty of writing reflectively for various audiences, particularly where assessment criteria are also part of these understandings. Portfolios may be available to managers, (informally or as part of appraisal), or academic assessors for accreditation. The writer of such an autobiographical narrative needs to know which parts of the document are private or public, and by what criteria the public parts will be judged.

Critical sociologists such as Edwards and Usher (1995) relate the development of portfolios to current widespread use of many education and learning tools (learning contracts, APEL, records of achievement) that expect students or employees to use personal material in their course work or work record. They class these tools as educational practices whose purpose is reveal hitherto private and personal aspects of an individual. The personal biographies are at the same time both private and public documents, available for inspection and assessment by managers and teachers. These inspections may result in academic and management decisions which could impact on the candidate or employee's career. Informal feedback shows that some students find reflective writing difficult, and can feel rather exposed by the more subjective nature of the material required. Their difficulty may be partly caused by the sense of vulnerability created by writing personally for assessment. This can be addressed by clarifying the ownership of various parts of the portfolio. Candidates can then make their own decision about which sections of the portfolio various audiences may read.

Implications for good practice

In this section, we draw upon the experience of practitioners and the theoretical issues to identify some points that we feel staff using portfolios as a teaching tool need to consider.

In our view, good practice would involve:

1 A clear, concise rationale and justification for the use of portfolios. This should indicate which sections will be made public and which sections can be kept private. Clarification of this would be useful to the course team and we feel should also be communicated to the candidates, perhaps as a preface to the portfolio.

2 Clear guidelines for users of the portfolio. Good examples are provided in the appendices.

3 Adequate tutor or mentor support. The tutor's role will involve:
   a) clarification of the task – although most portfolios do contain introductory sections, the tutor's advice is crucial here;
   b) holding formative tutorials in which students' work is monitored, goals renegotiated as necessary and appropriate feedback is provided;
   c) helping students to write reflectively. (As noted, this does seem to be an area many candidates find difficult. The tutor can help by clarifying the purpose of reflective writing and, when required, help the candidate locate suitable reading.)

The authors have found that tutorial groups provide a good way of achieving some of these aims. The peer group provides a useful forum to clarify expectations, discuss progress and also provide a supportive and motivating atmosphere. For further discussion, see Bloor and Butterworth (1991), and for a discussion of the tutorial support required when portfolios are used as part of a distance learning programme, see Butterworth and Edwards (1993).

4 Provision for both formative and summative assessment of the portfolio. The formative assessment will ensure that the candidate receives structured feedback from their mentor/tutor. The development of criteria for summative assessment clarifies the task as well as possibly providing an additional incentive for the candidate. These criteria should be published.

5   The possibility of an interaction between candidate's learning style and the portfolio requirements. Honey and Mumford have developed a model of learning styles from consideration of the Kolb model of experiential learning mentioned earlier in this chapter. The four learning styles (Activists, Reflectors, Theorists and Pragmatists) each relate directly to the stages of the Kolb cycle. So, for example, some candidates will have no preference for a reflective learning style; they may prefer the activist's or pragmatist's approach and these candidates may possibly experience difficulties in reflecting and in reflective writing (Honey and Mumford, 1982). The writers have successfully used the Honey learning styles questionnaire in portfolio development sessions to help candidates diagnose their strengths and weaknesses and also clarify the rationale of the portfolio approach.

Conclusion

Portfolios are increasingly part of post-compulsory education and training provision.

This chapter has looked at different types of portfolios and identified a set of common purposes:
- recording training and work experience
- planning professional and career development
- encouraging critical reflection
- linking theory and practice

We have also identified an important educative element, where portfolios form part of the process of professional socialization.

Our own evaluation and analysis of current examples, however, indicates difficulties in achieving the above purposes and feedback from students provides evidence for both the advantages and disadvantages of portfolios. On the positive side, candidates may experience an increased sense of professional identity and personal and professional confidence. Some report that the process of critical evaluation in particular has helped them with the more formal academic demands of their course study. On the negative side, some candidates find reflective writing unfamiliar and difficult. Unless the production of a portfolio stimulates genuine learning, the process becomes merely a longwinded collation exercise. The guidelines for good practice given earlier should help realize the positive potential of the portfolio for supporting effective professional development.

Appendix 1 Extract from Professional Development Record, Institution of Mechanical Engineers

The individual

Engineering provides an ever changing spectrum of challenge and opportunity. It is, therefore, *vitally important* for all engineers to be committed to their own *Continuing Professional Development* (CPD) to enable them to face those challenges and to take advantage of all opportunities as they arise.

All engineers need to develop and implement a CPD plan; to record CPD activities and to assess the benefits so that they shape their careers rather than simply react to events.

The employer

More and more employers are realizing that a competent work force is their most powerful asset. Encouraging employees to complete Development Records will help employers and employees to analyse *together* the development needs of the individual and to decide how they fit in with the employer's own business plans. Inevitably, employees who are striving for excellence in their careers will contribute to a successful future for their employers.

Professional Development Record

To assist engineers, of all ages, levels and disciplines to identify, plan and record their professional development, the IMechE has produced a Professional Development Record (PDR).

The format is an A4 ring-binder with ten separate sections - the illustrations show the introduction and the tabs for each of the section dividers, and the layout of one of the sections. Each divider carries guidance notes relating to the purpose designed record sheets which follow. A copy of the Guide to Continuing Professional Development is also included.

The PDR will be:

- a valuable aid to career planning;
- helpful when deciding *what, how and when* new skills should be acquired;
- a record of competences gained;
- an indicator of any changes that need to be made;
- a career long reference for CVs or biographies.

**Appendix 2 Introductory sections of Professional Development Diary,
Chartered Society of Physiotherapists**

Professional Development Diary – Introduction

i. Purpose The Professional Development Diary has several purposes:

a. for use by student and qualified physiotherapists. The term 'physiotherapist' refers to both groups;

b. to enable you to record and monitor your own professional development;

c. to help you to identify and evaluate what you have learned from your experiences as a physiotherapist to encourage you to become a 'reflective practitioner';

d. to help you collect and collate material for Professional Development;

e. to help you in the process of claiming academic credit for your post registration professional experience, for example, by means of the Credit Accumulation and Transfer Scheme (CATS) operated in Higher Education.

ii. Structure The Diary is in five sections:

Section One is mainly factual and is concerned with the recording of your physiotherapy experience since beginning the Diary. Your current job content should be included in this Section to provide an overall focus for the recording in later sections.

Section Two is a record of your contemporary learning, both formal and experiential. It is important to note that this is NOT simply a factual record of the courses you have attended. As we noted in 1.c., one of the aims of the Diary is to encourage you to reflect on your experiences so that you can identify the relevant learning which you have acquired in a variety of situations.

Section Three is concerned with the information needed to form a Personal Development Plan, and will relate to various Sections of the Diary.

Section Four is for use when you wish to claim either professional or academic credit for your learning. This Section outlines the various options which exist for claiming professional and academic credit. You will need to consider the evidence which you can produce to support any claim which you might wish to make.

Section Five is for storage of documentation.

Appendix 3 Extract from ENB Professional Portfolio – Purposes of the portfolio

Summary card 3 – ENB professional portfolio

The ENB Professional Portfolio is an integral part of the ENB Framework for Continuing Professional Education and the Higher Award. The Board encourages every qualified practitioner to keep a Professional Portfolio as a record and a means to help reflect on professional development.

The ENB Professional Portfolio has been designed to:

- help nurses, midwives and health visitors improve the quality of the care they provide for patients and clients
- enable practitioners to keep a record of their professional and personal development, professional experience and qualifications
- encourage practitioners to develop skills of critical and reflective practice by considering experiences in professional and personal life and evaluating the contribution those experiences make to professional development and to improvements in client care
- enable practitioners to develop a full picture of professional and personal experience, and qualifications
- provide a way to record the credits each practitioner accumulates through participating in continuing education activities
- help practitioners take responsibility for their own continuing professional education and development.

The Portfolio is the personal property of each practitioner. It has a number of distinctive features:

- it is a flexible document
- each person should use it in the way that best suits their professional needs
- it does not matter which section the individual starts with. Some may wish to start with their current job in Section 2 and others may want to start by recording their previous qualifications and experience in Section 1.

There are a variety of ways for nurses, midwives and health visitors to use the ENB Professional Portfolio:

- It is useful for practitioners to review their Professional Portfolio regularly, particularly at significant points in their careers, for example when thinking of changing post or taking part in a continuing education event.
- The ten Key Characteristics which form the basis of the Framework and Higher Award are a central feature of the Professional Portfolio. Practitioners should use the ten Key Characteristics and the detailed learning outcomes to analyse their practice and identify their learning needs.
- The Framework and Higher Award are based on a constructive partnership between the practitioner, manager and educationalist. Practitioners can use the Portfolio to discuss their professional role within the organization and

professional development needs with clinical, managerial and educational colleagues.

The Higher Award

Each practitioner who decides to index for the Higher Award will be required to maintain a Professional Portfolio. The Professional Portfolio has been designed to meet the specific needs of nurses, midwives and health visitors who are indexed for the Higher Award.

- The Portfolio enables practitioners to develop a learning contract based on the ten Key Characteristics.
- The Portfolio is the basis of the learning contract that practitioners develop with their manager and educational colleagues.
- The Portfolio has sections for practitioners to record the credits they gain towards the Higher Award.

6 Flexible learning in FE and the implications for teachers

Jenny Ware

Introduction

The purpose of this chapter is to examine the key features of learning support workshops, especially those concerned with the provision of literacy support. From these features will be drawn some issues, principles and approaches for staff development which are applicable to those who are currently teaching in a wide range of flexible learning environments. Examples of these are open learning, resource-based learning and drop-in workshops, as well as support workshops of various kinds.

A workshop provides a student centred environment designed to enable learning to proceed as confidently and autonomously as the student's capacities allow. It also seeks to stretch those capacities to the full. Students experience a more egalitarian relationship with their teacher than in a more traditional classroom, since his/her role is to support and not to lead. They normally learn in a setting with a social dimension. They may encounter the opportunity to make choices concerning their own learning and to select their own materials. There is often the right to come and go and move around at will. Indeed, many workshops are designed specifically as a 'drop-in' facility which is available at the moment of need. The curricular emphasis is upon the acquisition of skills.

This differs from traditional forms of teacher led education where students are normally taught in a whole class situation and respond to the authority and superior knowledge of their instructor. They lack many of the freedoms accorded to workshop students. Traditionally, the emphasis has been upon the acquisition of a body of knowledge, but with the advent of GCSE this has been less the case.

Student centred workshops developed during the 1980s, largely in response to the influx of unemployed young people who were not succeeding on traditional courses. Initiatives like CPVE, Vocational Preparation and BTEC were undertaken to meet the needs of such students and flexible learning environments were established to provide literacy and numeracy support for their studies. In the then ILEA, these manifested themselves early as communications workshops and subsequently appeared in the rest of the country as English/literacy and maths/numeracy workshops.

A further factor in the development of this new kind of learning environment was the continuous rise in demands being made upon citizens' literacy and numeracy skills by an increasingly technological society.

The more recent advent of GNVQs has reinforced the role of flexible learning workshops in colleges, since its emphasis upon teaching core skills in an integrated manner requires vocational tutors to deliver a curriculum in which they are not necessarily specialists. Students with language difficulties are therefore more than ever in need of individual specialist support. This need is often identified by means of a test administered to all GNVQ students during the induction period and may be recorded in the action plan drawn up at the beginning of the course. Vocational tutors may also identify students in need of special assistance.

Such a learning environment has also been perceived to be of value to Special Needs students. Since incorporation and the establishment of the Further Education Funding Council (FEFC) funding has been available for additional learning support, which includes provision for students learning in small groups or on an individual basis, where there is a demonstrable need and where this is not part of the student's primary learning goal (FEFC, 1994, a).

Incorporation is likely to affect workshop provision in other ways, too. The FE sector has now been set high recruitment targets and offered financial rewards for the retention of students, as noted in Chapter 1. This, as well as the potential within the newly incorporated colleges for closures, mergers and redundancies, has meant that colleges are increasingly regarding as prospective client groups those who have to date not participated in further education.

The consequence for the curriculum is a developmental pattern similar to that (described above) which originally gave rise to flexible learning support. This is the design, often in-house, of new courses specifically for the needs of these new client groups and follows the Return to Learn and Access traditions. This tendency has been authenticated and emphasized by FEFC funding regulations which allow such courses to run providing they are externally validated, for example through the national Open College Network (FEFC, 1994, a).

Initially such a client group may be drawn into colleges by a variety of means – Return to Learn, short taster courses, Adult Basic Education (ABE) schemes, basic community education courses, for example. In the current climate, colleges will further emphasize their efforts to attract them into mainstream education, not least because the FEFC requires a demonstration of student progression. The influx of such a clientele, usually adults and often with literacy and numeracy needs, will present a further challenge to flexible learning workshops and their staff. The picture is additionally complicated by the recent absorption by many colleges of the voluntary local ABE schemes, initiated and supported nationally by ALBSU. These were hitherto often supported locally by the LEAs by means of training, additional posts or other financial support.

All these factors are contributing to an increasingly complex picture as far as the delivery of communications support, language support and literacy and numeracy teaching are concerned.

The learning wants and needs of FE's clientele

The characteristics of students receiving language and basic skills support over a number of colleges that were studied by the author between 1986 and 1993 conform broadly to a general pattern. Students often tend to be from socially deprived areas and schools and often appear to be unsupported educationally at home; in some cases, learning has been disrupted by illness; many have left school at the earliest opportunity, sometimes have a record of truancy and often have difficulty in learning in general. Some students come from an ethnic minority. Some workshops also provide for learners with a Special Need (see above) and/or for mature students.

Special Needs students often benefit from their experiences in workshops and their presence in those of a number of colleges is in line with the current emphasis upon their greater integration into mainstream courses. A particular advantage to them is that the student centred approach will be familiar to them from their Special Needs classes, yet they are experiencing a different ethos where they have the opportunity for some independence from their usual courses and tutors.

Some workshops incorporate ABE schemes with volunteer tutors. There is a debate concerning the role of these tutors in such a context and some colleges have chosen to dispense with them and teach solely in groups. The main reasons for this have been doubts as to volunteer tutors' effectiveness in improving literacy skills and a concern that some students can become very heavily dependent upon the volunteers. However, students do not like to be taught in groups when they are trying to acquire basic literacy skills since they wish to concentrate specifically on their own needs and often in a private context. Nevertheless, if students are to progress, there is a need for careful attention to be paid to the moment when they move into groups and into more mainstream learning. This has not been a strong feature of the voluntary schemes in the past (Charnley and Jones, 1979).

These characteristics indicate further the breadth of the challenge facing workshop managers and teaching staff if they are to induce new motivation in learners who have often experienced only failure during their period in traditional education. As has been demonstrated, the influx of a new clientele is complicating the scene further.

The key features of flexible learning

An ideal environment for flexible learning is one which encourages informality. The purpose of such an ethos is to break down the traditional barriers between student and teacher which may have become associated with a sense of past failure, to help students to build self-confidence and to enable them to identify their own prior learning as a valid basis upon which to build. This approach also recognizes the important part that informal discussion has to play in learning. As one student put it, 'Linguistic ability is the basis of all study' (Ware, 1993, p.113).

This approach is also completely student centred in its focus upon the fulfilment of individual needs, working at the pace of individuals and tracking progress individually. Ideally the learning environment:

1 is physically organized so as to encourage communication; there are often octagonal tables enabling face-to-face communication between students and an egalitarian relationship with the teacher; there is usually no teacher's desk;
2 fosters informal relationships between students and teachers, facilitating conversation; this constitutes the essential basis for the development of written language;
3 encourages the intimacy of small group work; students are able to use their own familiar language patterns and, by means of joint engagement in new learning experiences, negotiate new forms of language to accommodate them; they are also able to support one another's learning and experience independence from the teacher;
4 enables students to develop confidence and maturity in their approach to learning with the ultimate goal of autonomy; this is achieved by a variety of means, including those in 1–7 and by the interaction between teacher and student;
5 makes provision for a learning agenda which is negotiated between teacher and student;
6 allows students periods of time without the teacher so they can establish their own group identity and interact with each other independently;
7 provides a wide range of linguistic experiences and tasks;
8 enables language to be taught in the context of the whole educational experience.

Attendance is normally voluntary in these workshops and, particularly where mature students are present, the atmosphere is usually very well motivated.

Learners feel they are being taught well and that their chances of success on their mainstream courses have been enhanced by attendance at the workshop.

Typically, such workshops operate in the following way.

The setting is a large room with mobile furniture, allowing flexibility; there is a discrete entrance to allow anonymity for those wishing it. The space is divided up by screens to provide privacy for those working on individual tasks and to cut down on noise, which can present a major problem. Tea and coffee are freely available. A choice of books and magazines at different reading levels is on show for students to choose from and there is a supply of tapes which can be used with worksheets in carrels equipped with earphones and tape recorders. Around the room, there are computers and clearly marked filing cabinets from which students can select appropriate learning materials.

Staff walk round informally providing help as and when required, taking care to observe students working in the more obscure spots. Simultaneously, timetabled groups may be working with a teacher at the tables provided for this activity. Adult basic education students may be receiving tuition from volunteer tutors in spaces around the room. Special Needs students may be learning either in small groups or with individual support.

In theory, the initial learning agenda is negotiated with the student and a form exists for this purpose; in practice, students have a tendency to succumb to the belief that 'Teacher Knows Best' and prefer to be teacher led. Sometimes, and more successfully, students are requested to keep a reflective diary of their learning experiences, which is confidential to themselves and their tutor. The latter is then able to provide appropriate, continuous support and to amend the learning programme accordingly.

Student progress is recorded on a profile which is kept accessibly with current work. As an alternative or supplement to choosing their own tasks, students may be allocated a tutor who corrects work between sessions and places suggestions for further activity in the files before the next session. This enables students to begin working independently as soon as they arrive. However, this approach places a large burden on staff and students often want to take their work home with them, so the system does not always succeed.

Teaching materials are preserved by means of a master file carefully guarded by the workshop manager. Updating and augmentation are usually the responsibility of the workshop team as a whole.

The strengths and weaknesses of flexible learning workshops

Apart from its organization, the great strength of this model lies in its ethos, which allows particularly non-threatening relationships to develop between tutors and students, enabling students to build confidence in their ability to learn.

Evidence that this can be very effective appears in learners' own statements that they are more highly motivated by the workshop environment and feel they are making more progress than they have experienced in previous educational contexts. The statements reported in this chapter were collected a series of investigations carried out between 1985 and 1993.

The workshop characteristics with the greatest significance as far as learners are concerned are the informality of the ethos and the non-threatening personae of their teachers who, conscious of the need to undo past negative experiences, are placing a high value on friendly and supportive relationships:

> ... The workshop is communal – homely – and the teachers are very good; they're prepared to work hard for you and are very patient with people who are struggling. (Ware, 1993, p.144)

> The atmosphere is 95% the teacher. There is a caring atmosphere; she's approachable and makes me feel that my point of view's worth considering. (Ware, 1993, p.144)

Students prefer the atmosphere in workshops to that in their other lessons and find it conducive to learning. They feel that their own performance is better in a workshop environment. Similarly, it has been observed that in voluntary ABE schemes, a student's acquisition of confidence has depended upon the warmth of the tutor's personality (Charnley and Jones, 1979).

Moreover, the knowledge that the learning experience is focused on their particular needs effects an increase in students' self-esteem. A further strength is the workshop's ability to allow students the satisfaction of directing their energies at their own perceived weaknesses in a private context. This last factor means that learners tend to have more clearly defined learning goals than students in a traditional classroom. The flexible nature of the arrangement also enables provision to be made for students at any level of need, from the very basic to the highly sophisticated.

A workshop is also an environment which, because it permits informal oral forms, validates students' own prior learning as a basis for further linguistic development, an important learning experience for individuals who may have suffered linguistic non-comprehension in the traditional classroom (Edwards and Giles, 1984). This strength is well illustrated by students' own statements about their experiences:

> In some lessons the teachers don't listen and don't explain; in the workshop they do... the teacher's standing by you rather than shouting at you from the front. At school it was a public performance every time you learned something. Here there's less pressure, so I can learn more. (Ware, 1993, p.117–118)

This informality also allows tutors to provide informal counselling and support. Charnley and Jones (1979) identified similar characteristics in volunteer tutors working in Adult Basic Education schemes.

Students also respond to the nature of the learning materials they encounter and enjoy tasks that help them to improve their 'everyday' English; they perceive this aspect of their study as helpful both at work and in their social lives: 'It helps me especially in arguments with my Dad' (Ware, 1993, p.117). Both a weakness and a strength of workshops lies in their voluntary nature. On the one hand, motivation is usually high because students have elected to come. On the other, ways have to be found to entice them there. One important requirement here is the awareness and support of other members of the college. The perceptions of vocational course tutors are therefore of considerable importance in their role as potential referrers of a large proportion of the prospective clientele.

In colleges with established workshops, vocational tutors often show supportive attitudes towards these when they are aware of their aims and are informed about their activities. A reverse side of this coin is that most vocational tutors do not perceive their own teaching role as having any relevance to the language needs of students and do not make use of the resource represented by teachers of language to check or modify the way in which they transmit their own subject matter to students. Failure or drop-out is usually accounted for by students' lack of ability whereas the real factor may be linguistic non-comprehension.

The main weaknesses of flexible learning workshops lie in the danger of isolating students with their individual tasks; this tendency can be exacerbated by their own strong commitment to this aspect of their development. The consequences may be an exaggerated emphasis upon writing. This would be at the expense of developing spoken language, a prerequisite in any case for the development of written skills (Hodge, 1981) as well as of autonomy in learning. That this is a general danger is evidenced by the observations of an ILEA advisory teacher in the early days of workshops there:

> I suppose [this is] one remove from the classroom situation... at least they are working at their own pace. But... it falls short of what a workshop should be about because... the group interaction... is much more educative than dependence upon the teacher. (FEU, 1981, p.34)

Far from encouraging a growth in learning maturity and autonomy – as evidenced in an increase in students' ability to contribute to one another's learning, for example – this approach may be reinforcing lack of confidence and dependency upon the teacher. The dangers of the extensive use of this approach have been noted elsewhere (Charnley and Jones, 1979). The loss of some of the potential advantages of the workshop environment are very evident and, in particular, the advantages of group tuition emerged strongly, as a means by which individual students were able to reassess their self-image. It became clear that there were severe limitations in one-to-one tuition in achieving the objectives of adult education (Charnley and Jones, ibid.).

For these reasons, whilst the approach may create the impression that power sharing is treated as an important part of the learning process, it is in reality strictly limited:

> ...some systems of individualized learning, while offering lip service to the concept of assisting the student to become autonomous, in fact reassert the teacher's control over the student by isolating him with his task... (FEU, 1981, p.34)

Students sometimes respond to this negatively but the fact often goes unrecognized by both teacher and student.

As has been pointed out, students do not always respond positively to notions of autonomy in learning. Mature students sometimes seek to bolster their self-confidence by deferring to the teacher's superior knowledge and expertise; students who have been experiencing one-to-one tuition on an Adult Basic Education scheme often do not wish to give up this comfortable and supportive relationship for the sake of progression. Workshop students also often state their preference for the security and convenience of this strategy. Amongst the 16–19 year-olds are often youngsters who do not have the necessary maturity and self-discipline to work without close supervision. Caught up in the 'teacher knows best' syndrome, students sometimes also feel unable to create their own learning agenda.

Further, there is evidence of a loss of opportunity in such an environment for sustained conversation. This seems surprising in a context where students are clearly comfortable in making many spontaneous remarks. However, whilst the more relaxed relationships encourage brief social noises, the functional approach to language development evinces a high level of teacher input and does not often lead to sustained discussion with or between students. Students' own oral contributions are often inhibited by their belief in the superiority of the teacher's knowledge. The traditional classroom situation with its teacher led emphasis upon class and small group discussion is clearly serving students' needs more fully in this particular respect. In this context, teachers are normally effective in the creation of a forum for the free exchange of ideas by the choice of sympathetic subject matter and the skilful use of questioning techniques. In a flexible learning environment, there is a tendency on the part of tutors to instruct individuals upon ways of improving, for example, their written language in a technical context, to the exclusion of other kinds of talk except for friendly chat to which the student often responds only briefly. Nevertheless, standard classroom dynamics often preclude the possibility of informal exchange and spontaneous comment and students who engage in these may be regarded as uncooperative. The two kinds of oral experience can be summed up as the difference between a domestic and a public situation. In that they make different demands upon their oracy, students are encountering vastly different learning situations. Each has something significant to offer the other in terms of teaching techniques and it is clear that in flexible learning workshops, there is a need for greater awareness of the importance of extending the opportunities offered to students to widen their oral experience.

A similar criticism can be made of the nature of the learning materials encountered by students. As has been illustrated above, students' own statements reflect a broad perception of the kinds of linguistic experiences that they wish to encounter. Although their main priorities for becoming more literate are functional (such as learning to cope with letters and forms, enhancing job prospects) students also place a high value on oracy, developing the ability to think more clearly and use of the imagination. These priorities are broader than the learning experiences offered by many of the workshops they inhabit, for the vast majority of teaching materials in many workshops narrowly focus upon functional literacy and sometimes specifically upon the world of work. Whilst there is an undoubted value in placing language development within realistic contexts and in enabling students to tackle tasks that are related to their needs in the 'real world', to do so exclusively would seem to be of dubious merit.

Elsewhere it is argued that the basis of language acquisition is the development of personal self-esteem and it has been noted that where volunteer tutors came to understand that experience of success was the key to learning, the 'training' as opposed to the 'education' element in the process tended to diminish in importance so that skills increasingly occupied a lower place down the scale of priorities (Charnley and Jones, 1979). In a 1994 CBI survey of the skills employees found lacking in applicants, literacy ranked ninth out of ten: it was the broader communication skills, including personal and interpersonal skills, that they considered to be missing (Clark, 1995). The development of literacy for private and personal purposes is a further important consideration (Lankshear et al., 1987).

Moreover, students themselves often wish to select their own learning contexts and sometimes do so, even where this is not done by means of a recognized and formal negotiation. Many students would appreciate the introduction of topics and ideas that are new to them:

It opens up my thinking and makes me aware of words and how you use them. Now I know you have to read things more than once, I can see them differently. (Ware, 1993, p.116)

Many students would like more opportunities to explore the use of their imaginations:

It makes my life feel more colourful and I have to think hard to find the right words to say what's in my head. (Ware, 1993, p.116)

Written materials and written tasks need to reflect the desire of many students to acquire language in a wider and/or more varied context than has hitherto normally been offered and also to take more account of the likely cultural interests and social class of their users.

Conclusion: approaches to staff development and suggested strategies

Workshops largely developed as a result of grassroots enthusiasm and energy and their form reflects teachers' responses to student need. This raises the question of who should normally be conducting staff development sessions and the answer will often be the staff themselves, and in particular, the workshop manager.

A further question concerns the selection of staff who might benefit from such development and training. Although this chapter has focused largely upon the development of language skills, the issues that arise from that debate are equally relevant to all kinds of flexible learning, for example open learning, resource-based learning, drop-in workshops, and the delivery of GNVQs. Therefore those in need of staff development and training might well be drawn from the whole range of the college's flexible learning provision. Indeed, those whose role is not primarily to enable language development could reasonably be expected to be less aware of the pitfalls of flexible approaches to learning. Therefore they might be considered to be in greater need of information concerning the linguistic prerequisites of successful learning in these contexts. Further, much of the good practice identified here (for example, the establishment of a non-threatening learning environment, learning in groups as well as individually, negotiating meaning through the medium of the students' own language, a negotiated learning agenda, non-directive verbal interactions, personal support for students, the provision of broad learning experiences and tasks and so on) has relevance to learning in general and is not specific to language development. The experiences and perceptions of staff drawn from across the college would be likely to make further contributions to the debate.

The establishment of networks (or consortia) across interested colleges would help to broaden horizons further, share problems and new ideas and to generate and exchange materials. Consortia, such as those set up to support the Mode Three GCSE courses, were so effective in their developmental activities that when these kinds of courses were superseded by Key Stage 4, the Southern Examining group (at least) encouraged them to continue. This would therefore appear to be a useful model to emulate. Further, this democratic approach to staff development is a reflection of the democracy such teachers are expected to achieve in a flexible learning environment.

As has been shown, the greatest strength of workshop tutors is the way in which they have succeeded in creating an environment that is attractive and reassuring to students who may have experienced educational failure in the past. To this extent, workshops are already highly student centred and their key elements negotiated, however broadly this may have occurred through tutors' accumulated experience of students' needs. There would therefore be a value in pursuing awareness raising activities in order to support the teachers' own abundant creativity. One way in which this could be achieved is by the informal sharing by practitioners of knowledge and experience across colleges. As has been demonstrated, these issues concern learning in a general sense and therefore most appropriately include staff from across the whole breadth of flexible delivery. More structured staff development sessions would need to be student centred so that teachers receive first hand experience of the strategies they are employing with students.

A fundamental issue is the importance of a redefinition of the term 'workshop' and, indeed, of flexible learning as a whole. These terms often have strongly utilitarian connotations in relation to learning and on occasion, they are also identified as cost-cutting activities, with the possible implication of more paper-based learning and less tuition, thus effectively reducing the verbal interactions between student and teacher and, potentially, between students, too. As has been demonstrated, the development of these interactions is central to learning and requires skill and understanding to implement. Failure to address the issue is unlikely to achieve a full realization of students' potential. The delivery of quality education in flexible learning contexts is therefore dependent upon the understanding of these issues by the deliverers.

These learning needs in students are recognized in some of the strategies used by schools and in GCSE and usually in 'A' Level teaching, but at lower levels of attainment in FE the recognition is sometimes lost in the concern to hasten the acquisition of competency in written skills. Staff development sessions would therefore need to consider strategies for the further development of students' oracy. In workshops where students always study individually, this would imply a restructuring of the system so that, from time to time the vast majority of students (except perhaps those who had come to learn a very specific skill) were able to experience strategies such as whole class discussion, small group work, debates, committees and other such activities.

A further related issue concerns the breadth of contexts within which students are encouraged to write. Collaboration between colleagues and also between colleges in the development of learning materials is a particularly useful way of achieving breadth, since experience and expertise are readily and efficiently shared during such practical activities. What is required most is an injection (into the frequently functional materials of sub-GCSE areas) of some of the GCSE style and approaches with their broader range of materials and tasks. Where language development is specifically the issue, these developments would be less likely to occur in workshops which are isolated from the rest of the English teaching in the college with its associated perspectives and expertise. These perspectives would again have importance for flexible delivery in its wider context. In colleges where general education is disappearing in favour of an exclusive offer of vocational education delivered through GNVQ and other forms of flexible delivery, these skills and perspectives are in danger of disappearing altogether from the FE curriculum. This would be all the more reason for networking with other FE colleges and even with schools.

Further, tutors need more information about the ways in which they interact verbally with their students. An apparently non-directive, egalitarian environment may in fact be unintentionally reinforcing dependency because of the teacher's directive verbal interactions with the students. Teachers could be encouraged, for example, to monitor one another informally by means of Flanders' Interaction Analysis. This instrument is designed to identify the level of direction in the verbal utterances that occur between student and teacher. It distinguishes between, for example, the amount of question and answer, the amount of lecture, the number of spontaneous utterances arising from students and the degree to which the teacher is building upon student comments and recognizing students' feelings. It would be a useful instrument for staff development purposes since it would empower staff to identify the issues for themselves and to decide for themselves what the remedies would be. It is also economical of time, since it is possible to collect useful information about an individual teacher's interactions in about twenty minutes. There is evidence to suggest that volunteer tutors, in particular, would benefit from this information about their communication.

There is also need for a closer consideration of strategies for the encouragement of students to take more responsibility for their own learning. The fundamental need is for a dialogue between tutor and student to which the student contributes with increasing confidence. Whether this occurs through the medium of a form, a confidential diary, discussion or by other means, the widespread view of students that 'Teacher knows best' needs to be broken down if growth in self-esteem and movement towards learning autonomy are to be achieved. Sharing experiences of means and methods would make a contribution to the improvement of this important aspect of students' learning.

The needs of young participants also require examination: in workshops where they are left largely to their own devices whilst the tutor(s) attend to a wide range of individual needs, much unproductive activity occurs. There may be a need to structure some sessions so that they cater for different kinds of clientele, offering a progression towards autonomy at a rate appropriate to a particular group. This would cut across the principle of constant access, but might offer a better service to all. Staff development sessions in many colleges may well need to address such issues.

Workshops are more effective in drawing in students in colleges where vocational tutors are aware of and support their philosophy, aims and methods. Opportunities for workshop staff to communicate these and to negotiate over them with vocational staff should be provided. Further potential lies in creating opportunities for vocational and language staff to discuss the language used in handouts and other teaching aids.

Time spent on these measures would be likely to increase recruitment, diminish student drop-out and enable learners to maximize the use of what may well be a very short last chance in education provided by their FE course.

Workshops were initiated in-house by FE staff, much of the initial development coming from the then ILEA Curriculum Development Project at Westminster College, London. To date, higher education has not played a prominent role in teacher training for workshops. Since flexible learning appears to be developing a higher profile and because there are gaps in existing practice, there would seem to be a clear case for training prospective teachers in workshop skills. As has been indicated, such skills will be increasingly required across a whole range of educational contexts in further education.

7 The role of the staff development practitioner in the FE college

Anne Castling

Introduction

Staff development is a vehicle for the management of change. It is the means whereby college corporations ensure that they have an appropriately trained and responsive staff capable of helping the organization meet the objectives in its strategic plan. Given that these objectives concern the provision of high quality learning opportunities for all those who can benefit from them, the staff development process, by supporting the staff in this corporate endeavour, is central to the mission of the college.

Staff development personnel, as key figures in the staff development process, must be seen as agents of change. Their role is predominantly to empower staff by helping them cope with internally and externally generated change.

In this chapter, we see how the role of staff development has evolved from its ad hoc beginnings to its present position within a quality assurance framework. We see a parallel development in the role of the staff developer. Trends in staff development in colleges since incorporation are explored together with the implications for staff development personnel. We look at a number of models of interesting practice, particularly the staff development team and staff development network. At all stages we see how the chief role of the staff developer is in promoting and mediating change in a context where the adaptability and flexibility of staff are their most valued attributes. The chapter draws on experiences in Southgate College (which may not be typical or ideal) and an attempt is made to generalize from these to help the reader apply the account to their own context.

The role of change agent

Staff developers receive their remit from the senior management team who are themselves responding to internal and external pressures for change. The orientation of the institution towards this change is of crucial importance. If the orientation from the top is positive, change will be seen as inevitable, necessary, stimulating, able to be anticipated, managed and to become a rich source of learning. Staff development will be seen as a focus for creativity, energy and achievement. Staff will be encouraged to grow, to adapt, and will be congratulated on doing so.

If the orientation from the top is negative, change will be seen as inevitable but threatening, a process to be coped with grudgingly, as if it got in the way of the real job. Staff development will be seen at best as a sweetener to a bitter pill, at worst as a necessary imposed evil.

It follows, then, that staff developers may be perceived by staff as part of the solution or part of the problem, as people who offer opportunities or who pose threats. In a positive climate, they are seen as people who offer time and space for the learning and practice of new skills, together with encouragement and reassurance. They help build confidence, they acknowledge progress. They do this on behalf of the institution by providing resources and structures for development, be they training sessions, consultations with experts, visits to observe progressive practice, and so on. Not infrequently, they also provide a listening ear and a degree of empathy. Many staff developers will be active in teaching or support roles, and so bound up in the same institutional imperatives as their colleagues. This increases their credibility and acceptability across the college generally.

The further education context

Staff developers in colleges work in a particularly challenging context. The complexity of the further education system is seldom fully realized even by many of those who work in it. The hallmark of FE is its diversity, a characteristic which derives from its history. It is not rational or linear; it did not spring fully formed from the mind of the DES, but grew in fits and starts and leaps and bounds in response to mainly local needs and opportunities.

In some areas, virtual 'monotechnics' grew up to service a single large industrial complex: by contrast, a rural centre might be the focus for all levels of course from basic education to degrees across a wide subject range. Progressive amalgamations brought together colleges of art, building, agriculture, business, fashion, music, engineering – each with its own peculiar sense of mission somehow subsumed into the larger whole. Some institutions were committed to second chance education, others pushed for high qualification rates and academic excellence. Whereas some centres pursued entirely vocational goals, others were concerned with lifelong learning and personal enrichment.

74

Within many FE colleges today, these diverse purposes remain, masked by an anodyne, all embracing mission statement, causing considerable tensions between and within departments. Since most change involves a shift of attitude or statement of value, these tensions can surface and become major stumbling blocks to development. This is clearly illustrated in the varying responses to the introduction of National Vocational Qualifications, or to the development of Access courses, the introduction of SLDD students into mainstream programmes, or indeed the use of the language of manufacturing to describe the education process.

In other words, colleges of FE are not businesses conveniently lined up behind a single purpose to which all staff would assent, unless it be so bland as to be meaningless in action. This has considerable implications for staff development, not least the difficulty of managing sessions with mixed groups drawn from these diverse 'mini cultures'. When facilitating development sessions, the staff developer is often engaged in helping (cajoling? wooing?) people to work towards a common purpose. They may find considerable energy is dissipated in explaining or justifying college policies! At worst, people may refuse to give their commitment; at best, the mix of values may lead to creative solutions.

The diversity in provision and student groups in FE which has resulted from this history of expansion and amalgamation can be bewildering to a newcomer. Here is a service which operates from 0830 to 2130 each day of the week to full time, part time, short course or sandwich students who can be aged from 14+ – 60+, can belong to any ethnic group, may live locally or be bussed in, may be studying at any level from basic to degree, may be self-employed, employed or unemployed, keenly motivated or shockingly idle, highly intelligent or barely able to cope with their course choice. On any given day they could be studying biology, beauty therapy, Bantu, brickwork, Boolean algebra, business studies, bakery or basketball!

This diversity of client group is an issue for staff development. Many staff will have been attracted to a college with the expectation of working with a particular kind of group in a given subject area. Because of the range of provision the work context of some staff will be radically different from that of others, so much so that they might almost be working in different institutions. This can be true particularly of those who only work 'the night shift', or where there are several college sites. The challenge for staff developers is to help them all meet their diverse needs within the framework of the particular activity, and to translate the objectives of the session into examples which will be meaningful across the various divides. How, for example, will the new achievement-based funding outcomes relate to students who cannot achieve even the lowest level of NVQ?

The characteristics of the staff themselves are similarly diverse. They may be on full time, part time or fractional appointments, temporary or long term contracts, new or old conditions of service, have 20 years experience or two, have teaching qualifications or none, come from professional, business, industrial or academic backgrounds, be aged anywhere between middle 20s and middle 60s, come from any ethnic background, and be on the teaching or the support staff.

Again, this is a staff development issue, or rather several issues. How is the staff developer to help them perceive the relevance of particular external or institutional expectations to their areas of work? How can the weary cynic and the rising star be linked in the same enterprise? How to prevent individual hobby horses and grievances taking over the agenda of sessions where debate is the vehicle for development?

All this diversity exists in a context which is itself changing rapidly. Virtually every aspect of the FE service has been undergoing continuous change for the past 20 years. There are new management structures (incorporation), a new paymaster (the FEFC), new funding mechanisms, new qualification structures, new philosophies, new modes of learning, new modes of communication, new conditions of service, new administrative systems, new regulations, new course structures, new client groups and new accountabilities.

This is the context in which staff development functions. Sheer overload of information and ideas can create blocks to development even in the most motivated staff. For developers themselves there is the need to have a grasp of the whole picture in order to help colleagues to appreciate their part in it. They will need to explain, if not justify, key developments and to do so repeatedly in difficult areas. It will be particularly important to strike the right note. Staff already stressed by the pace of change may construe suggestions that they undertake professional development as criticism of their current job performance, and fear to embark on needed development work in case it be perceived by others, especially senior staff, as an admission of failure. It behoves staff developers to be particularly sensitive to staff vulnerabilities. The role of the staff developer is not just to carry out agreed functions, but to carry them out in very particular ways.

The developing concept of staff development

It will be apparent from the previous analysis that staff development is not merely an administrative function, not direct training, though it includes both of these, but a complex of processes carried out within interlocking relationships. Whereas the staff development systems may be tidily objective, staff development process are much more of an art than a science. This has always been the case, but the changing pattern of staff development itself over the last 20 years, and essentially the last five years, has made this much more apparent. The staff developer is no longer a functionary – s/he is a designer, interpreter, mediator. Surprisingly s/he has become all of these things as the systems themselves have become increasingly more standardized. A brief survey of key stages in the evolution of staff development will show how this is the case.

The early days of staff development in the 70s were exciting times for developers, often entrusted with a budget of up to £2000 and two hours a week remission to design and operate a system for the whole college. Initially the emphasis was on induction for new staff, initial teacher training, mentorship, career guidance and subject updating through attendance at external courses.

Gradually an awareness grew that external courses were not the full story, that the job itself was rich in developmental possibilities. This was a discovery much assisted by a continuous stream of projects lodged in colleges by the then Further Education Unit during the 1980s. These enabled staff to pilot all manner of strategies related to key college processes – recruitment, marketing, course evaluation, integrated IT, equal opportunities, credit accumulation systems, and so on.

Developers themselves tended to be homegrown, untrained for their role of designing and implementing staff development systems, and frequently peripheral to strategic planning and decision making. [1] They came from varied backgrounds, many of them from teacher training, general or communication studies , or as appointments under specially funded Manpower Service Commission Training Schemes for the unemployed.

When, in the 1980s, LEAs took over the management of earmarked funding related to government determined national priorities for staff development, the service rapidly became more systematized. HMI ran national conferences to induct staff developers into needs analysis and aggregation for bidding purposes. The National Association for Staff Development, through its twice yearly journal and conferences programme, provided support and development for its own practitioners consistently over the period. The staff development officer in the college was now involved in assessing needs, planning programmes against specified outcomes (related to the college strategic plan), managing the bidding process, organizing the running of the programmes, and evaluating their effectiveness. For the first time there was a realistic, even generous, budget.

There were some disadvantages to the government funded budgets, the worst being the exclusion of support staff from the funding, clearly a complete nonsense which had to be circumvented in various ways. It was also difficult to secure adequate resources for local priorities (as opposed to national), and the need to submit bids 18 months in advance reduced responsiveness. Evaluation consisted almost entirely of counting training days.

But the legacy of the various budgets with their now fading acronyms – TRIST, GRIST, LEATGS, GEST – was largely positive. Apart from producing much more targeted activity with stated outcomes linked to strategic plans it also, because of the much higher profile given to staff development by the availability of a realistic budget, raised staff expectations. Far more people were participating in staff development, much of it offered via innovative opportunities – projects, secondments, visits, exchanges, use of high quality consultants etc. This expectation of involvement in staff development continued into the late 1980s although the budget gradually diminished.

The role of the staff developer during this period included liaison with LEA officers responsible for managing the bids and evaluating the programmes. This could be a difficult relationship where LEA officers were less experienced and involved than their college counterparts. Certainly one of the key skills developed by the college personnel was that of designing provision to match their own particular context. However standardized the system, it remains true that each organization needs to impose its own style on the process if it is to attract and convince its own staff. The institutional ethos is very powerful – schemes do not necessarily transfer from one organization to another, even though the components might be, and indeed were largely similar.

Nevertheless, during this period, and indeed, since, the focus and content of staff development provision has become established. Most colleges have offered:

- support for newly appointed staff through programmes of introduction, induction and mentorship
- entitlement to initial teacher training
- job related middle management training
- senior management training, largely through participation in FE Staff College programmes
- refreshment of work experience through short secondments
- preparation for new institutional roles and responsibilities (e.g. personal tutorship)
- awareness raising in relation to legal responsibilities (e.g. health and safety, equal opportunities)
- training in the application of information technology to education
- training or support in relation to new approaches to teaching and learning.

Following incorporation [2]

Following incorporation, staff development has come to be seen as a service, the role of which is to help the college fulfil its mission by ensuring a suitably informed, trained and responsive staff. There is a much greater emphasis on institutional rather than individual needs; although personal professional development has not disappeared, it is now typically subject to careful scrutiny and a modest budget.

The role of line managers in the staff development process is strongly reinforced by placing staff development within a quality assurance framework which operates at individual, faculty or department and college level. Senior line managers, who are usually responsible for staff recruitment and career guidance are also often now involved in staff development through their appraisal activities.

Responsibility overall for staff development often lies with a senior post holder who is responsible also for quality assurance, within a broad remit for Human

Resources. Staff development is typically seen as contributing to a college's whole approach to quality; it cannot now be seen as an 'add on'. Commitment may be expressed through a staff development policy offering all staff various entitlements to appropriate professional development throughout their college career, including initial teacher training, subject updating and developmental appraisal.

The annual programme of staff development offered to staff may well be based on objectives in the strategic plan and annual operating statement. It is likely to have been created through consultation with senior line managers and to use feedback from staff participants in the previous annual cycle. In this model, all activities will have specified outcomes and be designed for particular target groups.

The budget is now likely to be allocated to programme areas on the basis of college priorities and external imperatives (e.g. NCVQ requirements for staff to be trained as assessors and verifiers). A proportion of the budget may be devolved to senior line managers, for the purposes of subject up dating, for example. The rest is probably managed centrally.

The offer to staff will be varied, and may include opportunities for work teams to design their own development schemes, for which they may be able to bid for funding. Work shadowing, visits, consultation with experts, course team projects and meetings, workshops and traditional courses are examples of the activities that may now be encouraged.

The staff development process is likely to be supported by a central administrative system which records involvement and spending, and whose data can be used for analysis as part of evaluation.

It is usual for the complete programme and all activities to be evaluated in consultation with participants both at the time and through follow up interviews which seek to establish the effectiveness of the development work in practice. Feedback on the value of staff development may also be gathered through the appraisal, course review and quality team processes.

In summary, contemporary staff development in colleges is likely to be:
- funded from the college budget
- managed by a senior post holder
- located within human resources management
- closely related to quality assurance
- based on work-related needs
- responsive to strategic objectives
- based on outcomes
- targeted
- offered to all staff
- monitored in the short term
- evaluated in the longer term
- externally inspected
- subject to audit.

The role of the staff development practitioner post incorporation

In-house staff development provision
There is one other major trend in staff development provision nowadays which has changed and expanded the role of the staff developer and that is the move to mainly in-house provision. Incorporation led colleges, inevitably, to look inwards. It also led to a search for cost effective systems. Externally based staff development had become very costly, as HE institutions and independent consultants, misled by the years of generous LEA funding, scaled up their prices. In-house provision began to look attractive in money terms.

A powerful advantage of in-house provision is the availability of the staff development practitioner to operate it. In addition, it is perceived to be:
- cheaper – so more people can have a share of the total budget
- relevant – no time wasted in translating from one context to another
- on the spot – no time wasted in travel
- targeted – precisely geared to individuals or groups
- responsive – to immediate as well as long term needs.

An added advantage is the opportunity to acknowledge the value of work done by staff, using them as expert witnesses within the programme, whereby they offer their own strategies for success to their peers.

Care has to be taken that potential difficulties with the system are avoided. There is the risk of staff becoming bogged down in institutional problems which can obstruct progress, and there may be a lack of fresh ideas which would normally come from working with colleagues elsewhere. There might be a reluctance to resource the input by college staff as fully as that by outside experts, and indeed college staff might not command the respect which would have been accorded to visitors purely because they were from outside. The chief danger is probably insularity. The staff developer managing the programme will need to import wider views, either from their own research or by selecting colleague contributions carefully.

Advantages having been seen to outweigh disadvantages, staff developers moved into the roles of in-house trainers and facilitators, leading events and organizing activities across a wide range of areas. They were not expected to be expert in the curriculum area themselves, but by consultation and research aimed to gain sufficient understanding to organize appropriate development activities. Their expertise lay in planning and setting up such programmes. As a result the organization was now in a much better position to own and control its professional development processes.

There were two immediate effects of this move to in-house provision. Staff's perception of staff developers changed. They were seen less as administrators, more as general advisers on a whole range of curriculum and institutional concerns. They were sometimes seen as more approachable than busy line managers to whom the same concerns might have been brought, and, more importantly, less judgemental. You could ask the staff tutor for help without the risk of being seen as a failure. A great deal of development work was generated 'on the hoof' as staff tutors walked the corridors or sat in common rooms. This had the effect of helping to knit staff development into the everyday life of the college, reducing ideas of remoteness or imposition.

It is unproductive to try to quantify or put boundaries round this general advisory function, where a simple enquiry can move to career counselling in minutes. Sometimes it is indistinguishable from the normal helpful staffroom interchange. At other times the trained listening and confidentiality offered by the staff tutor is of greater value to the recipient than might be anticipated. It is certain that by behaving helpfully in a routine, undramatic manner staff developers are acting as advocates for their service, making it more likely that staff will pursue more specific activities when need arises. This daily commerce acts powerfully to create the positive orientation towards change described earlier. It also, incidentally, imposes an obligation upon developers to be 'in role' during most encounters with staff, and an equal obligation not to vent any negative feelings of their own. If the developers can't be positive in troubled times, then what hope is there?

The second effect of the move to in-house provision was the need for monitoring and evaluation to become more systematic. Given that so much of the provision was under direct control, it was an easy next step to ensure all activities, whether designed by staff tutors or generated by staff teams, had statements of objectives and outcomes against which they could be evaluated. This helped to reduce sloppiness or complacency concerning standards of provision, and matched the prevailing tome of quality assurance itself, the one reinforcing the other. This is not the place to analyse staff development evaluation systems; it is sufficient to say that by setting targets, monitoring progress and reviewing longer term effect on practice, staff tutors increased markedly the credibility of their service in the eyes of colleagues and external assessors. By carrying out evaluation face to face, through discussion, interviews, faculty meetings and consultation with staff at all levels across the institution they contributed to the embedding of quality assurance processes. Indeed, it is at the evaluation stage that learning and progress is perceived by participants, which makes the evaluation itself a major developmental tool. [3]

Best practice in the 1990s – The staff development team
It should have become apparent from the preceding analysis that no single person could or indeed should, be the focus of these many aspects of the staff development practitioner's role. Given the complexity of college purposes, the range of demands for change and the sheer volume of people, the staff development team is the only viable solution.

The ideal team per se does not exist since teams can only be ideal in their own context. The model described below has been found effective in my own college to deliver an extensive programme and its evaluation.

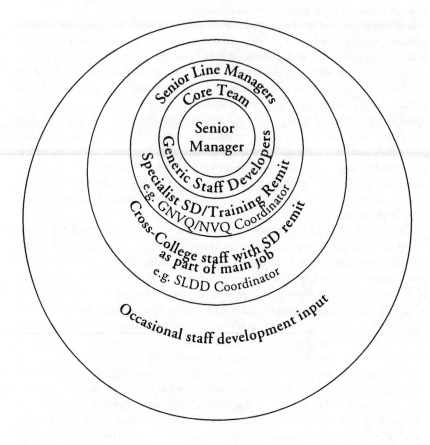

Figure 7.1   The Staff Development Team

Basically, there is a core team responsible for the design, delivery and evaluation of the college's staff development provision. There are then a series of outer circles or sub teams with greater or lesser responsibility. Core team members are generic staff developers, capable of carrying out all processes. Outer circle members have specific staff development responsibilities in relation to cross-college functions or curriculum areas. In a circle of their own but closely linked to the core team are the senior line managers. The Director of Human Resources (DHR) is the overall manager of the team, supported by her administrator.

Some notes on the team members

Senior Manager Responsible for policy; secures budget; is accountable to the corporation; directs the team; manages the team's work of planning, delivery and evaluation; reports to corporation and external agencies.

Senior Line Managers Responsible to Director of Human Resources (DHR) for professional development of their staff through selection, appraisal and support; approve individual staff action plans and choice of staff development activities: control devolved budget re subject updating etc., liaise with DHR and core team.

Generic Staff Tutors Help to plan the annual programme in consultation with staff and key post holders; manage cost centres; deliver activities; evaluate activities; offer general support and guidance; move around activity areas year by year.

Specialist Staff Tutor/Trainer Responsible for a current major priority area e.g. GNVQ/NVQ coordination; designs, delivers, evaluates training in this area. (Could also be ITT coordinator, Senior Management staff development coordinator).

Specialist Staff with an SD remit Hold cross-college roles with responsibility for SD in these areas (e.g. Personal Tutoring, Health and Safety, SLDD); work with a generic staff tutor to deliver SD in their activity area.

Occasional Staff Developers Staff whose role has college-wide implications who will work with a generic staff tutor to run occasional targeted sessions e.g., APL coordinator, Marketing Officer.

Staff Witnesses Any member of staff who is invited to witness to development work undertaken; facilitate training of colleagues because of particular expertise.

Staff Development Administrator Responsible to DHR, responsible for recording and manipulating data for its use in monitoring and evaluation; responsible for clerical backup services.

The core team also operates as a quality team in that it sets its own performance targets in relation to its various functions, monitors its effectiveness through feedback from staff across the college, and reviews its own operation in regular meetings. This process is organized by the more senior of the generic staff tutors who also has a quality assurance remit under the Director of Human Resources.

The wider view – the staff development network
A logical extension of the team is the network, which can be local, regional or national. The chief function of networks, according to research carried out by Don Scott of the National Association for Staff Development for the FEU (FEU, 1989), is to offer mutual support to their members. They do this by providing up to date information, a framework for debate, typically a journal or newsletter, and opportunities to share/gain expertise through meetings and conferences, face to face or by means of electronic media. The most effective at national level are the former Further Education Unit, the former Further Education Staff College (these two now being reconstituted as the Further Education Development Agency), and the National Association for Staff Development. [4] Regional Advisory Councils have been instrumental in setting up networks in their areas for groups sharing functions or curriculum areas. These also publish materials.

Local networks can provide far more frequent face-to-face contact for staff developers. They are variously organized and funded depending on the imagination and resourcefulness of their founders. I have been instrumental in running two very different networks, one in the North East of England in the 1980s , one currently in North London. There are lessons to be learned from each.

The Northern Region Staff Development Network (NRSDN) NRSDN was set up on a self help model with no funding and volunteer organizers and participants. Some 30 or so variously designated people with a staff development, educational development or staff training remit met about six times a year, hosted by their organizations in turn (a room and coffee!), sharing ideas and learning from each other's practice. We were deep into NTI (New Training Initiative-based staff development) which was making huge demands on our staff. As so often, the local HE organizations, Newcastle Polytechnic and Durham University's School of Education, offered accommodation, interest and practical support. The Polytechnic funded the publication of the Network's Proceedings under the entirely appropriate name Small Scale and Homespun.

This network succeeded because of shared need and a willingness to cooperate with, and to learn from, others. It was very much a child of the early DIY staff development culture!

The North Circular Staff Development Network This was set up in 1989 as a collaboration between six North London Colleges and the then Middlesex Polytechnic, now University. A pre-existing collaboration based on the Certificate in Education (FE) had been in place for some years, and some members worked across both teacher training and staff development functions. Both when it was set up and when it was relaunched more formally in 1992, the Network had a set of objectives, a measure of funding, staff with a small amount of time officially designated to work in it, systematized planning, delivery and evaluation mechanisms, an obligation to report to senior mangers and to manage its budget effectively. This degree of formalization is not surprising given that we are now in a much more hard edged climate. What is perhaps surprising is the commitment to collaborate and cooperate in a climate of ever increasing competition between neighbouring establishments. This reveals a degree of maturity and strong commitment to the basic staff development values of sharing and support.

The principles of fairness and mutuality are carried through in the Network's organization. One centre contributes the coordinator and another her assistant in any given year; the assistant takes over in the following year, shadowed by an assistant from a third centre, and so on. Meetings rotate around the centres so all are included during the year (a room and coffee!). Centres contribute the same sum (£1000) to a budget for the year, and there are no fees or accommodation charges levied on any centre.

However, this network is a working group charged with mounting six staff development events each year. These will fall into one or more of the following categories:

- too expensive to be mounted by any single college;
- a minority need, not likely to be met in college SD programmes;
- a successful event, area of high demand where repeats have been requested;
- an event for staff developers to help them with the information/skills they need for their own job;
- an event running in one of the colleges which staff from other centres could also attend to make it more cost effective;
- an event best run outside any of our colleges because of potential sensitivities or the need for confidentiality, and so on.

This network is also a success story, not solely in that it extends staff development opportunities in the sub-region but also because it is a small triumph of cooperation, putting into practice the need to respond positively and with imagination to the ever increasing demands for change which we all face.

The sum of the parts

The modern staff developer has a complex role, as we have seen, poised interestingly between management and staff, committed to empowering staff on behalf of the institution and its objectives. It is a role which requires a wide range of interpersonal skills since it is first and foremost based on direct relationships with staff. It also requires high levels of energy and organization, not a little imagination and a capacity to monitor one's own behaviour. Above all, it calls for a positive orientation towards change, based on a strong belief in every individual's capacity for growth in a supportive environment. Given that these are exactly the attitudes and capabilities we as teachers and managers want to develop in our students, there should be a close correlation between the roles of the developers and the developed.

Notes

1   The National Association for Staff Development (NASD) Working group on TDLB standards made reference to these aspects of the traditional situation of the staff development practitioner in 1991.
2   Throughout this description I have relied heavily on the system which is in place at Southgate College and which was recently validated by the FEFC Inspectorate. The pattern would, however, be repeated up and down the country to a greater or lesser degree.
3   Details of the Southgate College Staff Development Evaluation System are available from the author.
4   Details of NASD's twice yearly Journal and annual conference programme are available from the Hon. Secretary, Don Scott, 30 St. Helens Road, Colchester, CO3 3BA.

8 Investors in People: developing the people and developing the college

Margaret Adams

Introduction

This chapter has been written from the perspective of a consultant who is currently supporting educational establishments through the Investors in People (IiP) development process. The writer has worked with a number of colleges over the period 1992–1995 and has drawn on her experiences in colleges post-incorporation in defining the main themes of this chapter.

The chapter examines two major issues surrounding the implementation of the IiP quality management system in further education colleges in the mid-1990s. These are:

- the importance of IiP in helping colleges to succeed as businesses;
- the scope for, and limitations of, the staff development role in college development programmes leading to IiP recognition.

Throughout the chapter, the IiP standard is endorsed as a means by which staff development practitioners can both support the business development of the organization in which they work and fulfil their responsibilities to the ongoing development of the staff of their college, be they full time, part time or sessional staff, teaching, managerial or business support employees.

The chapter concludes that IiP is a useful quality standard for staff development practitioners and further education managers generally to adopt when they are supporting institutional and individual development, whether or not formal recognition as an Investor in People is sought by the college itself.

Investors in People

Investors in People is the National Standard for effective investment in people. It remains a Training and Enterprise Council (TEC) owned and TEC driven initiative which focuses on organizational development through the medium of the effective management and development of the organization's staff. Organizations which work towards that standard do so in order to be more effective when conducting all aspects of their business.

IiP is about improving performance and profitability through the appropriate utilization of the abilities of the organization's employees and through the development of skills within the entire work force that will help that work force to meet the changing demands of the business environment in which they are working.

The national standard implicitly endorses the belief that the people who work within an organization are the only sustainable source of its competitive advantage. Thus, investment in people is the most effective means of achieving business success. The national standard is built on four principles, those of commitment, planning, action and evaluation. In summary, these principles focus managerial activity upon the following elements:

Commitment *An Investor in People makes a public commitment from the top to develop all employees to achieve its business objectives.*

This principle defines an approach to people management and formally links the contribution of people to the success of the business.

Planning *An Investor in People regularly reviews the training and development needs of all employees.*

Although this principle addresses training and development, these needs are to be defined in terms of what the business requires in order to fulfil the objectives in its business or strategic plans.

Action *An Investor in People takes action to train and develop individuals on recruitment and throughout their employment.*

This principle deals with two distinct areas: training and development. In simplistic terms, training may be defined as off-the-job learning and development and development may be defined as on-the-job learning and support. This IiP principle encompasses significantly more than formal training programmes.

Evaluation *An Investor in People evaluates the investment in training and development to assess achievement and improve future development.*

This component is about the return on the investment in training and development. Organizations cannot simply build on the assumption that training and development are good things in themselves. The benefits to the organization utilizing training and development activities must be proven at the level of the individual, the team, or sub-institutional level, and at organizational level.

Investors in People in the further education context

Many further education colleges have made formal and public commitments to achieve IiP recognition. However, of the 1,700 or so organizations recognized as Investors in People by mid 1995, only about 20 are colleges.

However, IiP as a standard for people management and development is an appropriate quality development instrument for colleges to adopt since it is essentially about the key activities of:
* setting and communicating organizational goals and objectives to all staff;
* developing all staff to meet those goals and objectives.

The extent to which colleges have, in their IiP programmes, progressed with embedding these two key activities in their managerial activities varies enormously. Some have endorsed these principles unequivocally, and for staff development practitioners in such colleges, the IiP standard presents an excellent opportunity for them to embed staff training and development activities into the daily life of the college. The link between people development and the achievement of business and strategic objectives has been effected by colleges where the key activities associated with IiP, as identified above, have been understood and acted upon.

In the case of many colleges, the decision to make the commitment to IiP has necessitated some major shifts in perceptions about the role of staff development and its contribution to the overall success of the college. Where staff development, for example, has been perceived as a component of curriculum development alone and where the belief that professional people simply need regular updating of skills to sustain their expertise prevails, the journey to IiP status is longest and most tortuous. In such colleges, staff development sits at the margins of managerial concerns because the issues associated with the life cycles of qualifications, and with wholesale reskilling have yet to be explored.

For a number of colleges, the realization that recognition as an Investor in People will require significant organizational change has come some time after the commitment to seek IiP status has been made and in these colleges the task of gaining recognition has been redefined long after proposals have been sent to the local TEC.

Yet for colleges and staff development practitioners alike, the National Standard, once endorsed, presents opportunities to:
* develop all employees in line with business needs;
* sustain individual employee's expertise in a changing world of employment opportunities.

Thus:

> Investors in People is a remarkable source of support to all those involved with staff training and development. The initiative itself is unequivocal about the role and function of people and their development. They are at the heart of all successful businesses' strategies. (Adams, 1995, p.15)

The development processes which need to be undertaken in colleges to achieve such recognition contribute individually and collectively to the strength of the organization. Colleges recognize in increasing numbers that, by encouraging good business practice, these processes may help colleges to survive in an increasingly competitive education and training market place.

Investors in People and quality development

As a quality standard, IiP is an exciting vehicle by which FE colleges can ensure the place of staff development within their strategic management concerns. It is also a means of lessening the isolation felt by many staff development practitioners. All IiP programmes aim to help an organization achieve the national standard through the effective deployment, development and motivation of its employees; in this way, they support staff development planning, delivery and evaluation activities.

Further, the IiP development processes support college strategic planning and business management activities undertaken in line with the Further Education Funding Councils' (FEFC) requirements. The application of these processes guides the preparations for FEFC inspections by defining a rationale and business framework for all staff development activities. These are the same processes which encourage employee motivation through a commitment to lifelong learning and continuous development, in the context of organizational needs, that are found in all IiP organizations.

To gain recognition, all organizations must undertake the following processes:
- a commitment to achieve the national standard;
- diagnosis or audit with reference to the national standard;
- action planning;
- implementation of the action plan;
- assessment with reference to the National Standard;
- recognition as an Investor in People by the local TEC.

The implications for effective college management and for staff development as each part of the quality development process is addressed are significant.

Commitment to Investors in People

This is a public statement on the part of the organization to attempt to achieve a publicly endorsed national standard. The IiP award is recognized as a sign of commitment to continuous improvement and of a desire to achieve excellence. The initiative itself requires that such commitments be made unequivocally and from the very top of an organization. The impact of this commitment within colleges should be to focus managerial action on the achievement of what has now been defined as an organizational goal. Key players in supporting the achievement of this goal are the human resources and staff development personnel. If ever a staff development team sought an opportunity to have its

90

role and contribution to the effective management of the college recognized, a commitment to achieve the IiP standard delivers such an opportunity.

Diagnosis or audit
One of the most useful quality development activities is the IiP diagnosis or audit. It sits well with FEFC requirements for colleges to undertake self-assessment activities in preparation for their inspections, and the use of employee perception investigations is becoming more widespread in all sections of the economy, as a means of addressing a range of people management issues.

In the early days of IiP, the diagnosis was usually done for colleges via TEC supported consultancy. More recently, collaborative approaches to diagnosis (using a range of self-assessment and in-house investigations) have become more common. Consultants will often now work more closely with their clients, by supporting the development of the college's awareness of its own people management issues, rather than by undertaking all diagnostic activities on its behalf. For some colleges, this investigation will represent the first occasion on which such detailed information about employee perceptions has been sought, and in many cases, it will be the first time that the assertions of managers about the role of people and the benefits of training have been actively tested with reference to the perceptions of other employees in the same organization on such a large scale.

In terms of quality development, whether the outcomes of this activity are used to support preparations for an inspection or to support the activities of business development and college management, a valuable contribution will have been made. Information, analyses and conclusions, based on data drawn from the real college working environment, are produced whenever an IiP diagnosis is undertaken in a sympathetic, systematic and unhurried way.

Action planning
The IiP action plan defines what a college needs to do to achieve recognition as an Investor in People. Colleges' plans are produced with reference to the IiP assessment indicators and translated into key activities via summary statements, implementation programme outlines and management or executive summaries of the whole plan. In some cases, these documents will be produced by the consultant supporting the college; in other cases, college managers themselves will effect the plan's translation from the language of the assessment indicators into clear project management guides for individual managers to follow. Whatever form they take, they constitute a map for organizational development.

As noted by Adams (1994), the typical projects and activities that will emerge in action plans are those associated with:
• defining and communicating organizational goals to all employees;
• helping all employees to understand the nature of their contribution to the success of the college as a whole;

91

- defining the role and function of training and development in the college;
- confirming line management responsibilities in the context of people development;
- addressing communications issues within large organizations generally;
- matching business imperatives and human resource management activities for the benefit of the business;
- establishing and proving that there is a return on the investment in people.

The emphasis in each case will be different, of course, and the above list is by no means exclusive.

Staff development practitioners' inputs to this process can effectively guide the definition of development programmes. Through their inputs, they should seek to ensure that responsibility for the fulfilment of the defined activities is rooted in line managers' responsibilities rather than in the human resources, staff development or personnel functions. The staff development practitioner can become a skilled guide and adviser. Yet, that role holder should neither accept the sole responsibility for achieving IiP for the organization nor advocate that it should be delegated to any group other than the organization's line managers. It is only through the involvement of all managers, and not simply those fulfilling specialist functions, that steady and measurable progress towards IiP recognition will be made.

All of the above will contribute to the achievement of quality development objectives. Moreover, in the context of individual professional development and the development of all employees, colleges which address these issues are helping employees to know precisely what is needed of them in their current jobs, if they are to achieve and sustain competence.

It is in this context that issues of employability and realistic career profiling or career management are also raised. If a college has accurately assessed the demands of the economic environment in which it exists, then by defining the expertise it needs in its employees and by indicating the numbers of employees needed to deliver particular components of its service, it is publicizing what expertise individuals need to remain in employment and, by their omission from the definition, what skills that employer, at least, no longer needs. These activities communicate important messages to staff development practitioners and other employees alike, as employers may no longer be in a position to guarantee continuing employment for all staff. They should, however, be able to help all their employees address issues relating to their ongoing employability and thereafter, to help their employees sustain that employability whilst they are working for a particular college.

Implementation
This is the most difficult activity of all. IiP implementation is essentially about quality and organizational development. The action plan will have set out how IiP would be achieved, who will take responsibility for particular projects and activities,

92

how such activities will be resourced and over what time scale the whole project will be completed. IiP implementation is about fulfilling these commitments.

The project must, in this phase, be driven forward by committed individuals and by those who have the power in the organization to effect major change. Colleges are fortunate when such enthusiasm and power to effect change rest in the same group of individuals. However, the staff development practitioner, as an expert in people development, has an important role to play in supporting the whole process.

Those in further education with project management experience will know how difficult it is to keep staff focused on time bound objectives when teaching, curriculum development, FEFC imperatives (including inspections) and a range of local issues intervene. The task of the IiP team is to convince managers and all busy people in the college that their own objectives will be met more readily if IiP objectives are advanced.

Convincing busy managers that benefits will accrue to them if they change the way they are working is a difficult concept to establish, especially as there is never time to complete activities to individual's satisfaction anyway. Yet, in the end, it is only those managers who have credibility in managing the delivery of the colleges' various programmes and services who can endorse the beneficial effect of an IiP development programme. Staff development personnel, like all functional managers, can only do so much.

Organizational change brought about by the involvement with IiP may, for example, necessitate directing staff to develop particular skills, or introducing a system of performance management which evaluates formally how an individual is contributing to the achievement of the organization's objectives. It may even necessitate ensuring that all staff accept that as well as taking responsibility for the effective delivery of a curriculum to a group of learners, they also have responsibilities to serve their employing organization.

These will be major tasks, given the enormity of change required of some colleges, and it is not surprising that preparing the portfolio of evidence sometimes becomes the chief concern and the focus for activity in the implementation phase. The larger, and more difficult, organizational change and development issues may be put off until the nominated deadline for assessment approaches. The ramifications of this strategy need not be stated here.

Assessment

Investors in People assessment is organized by and delivered through the local TEC. Colleges which feel they are ready to be assessed against the National Standard will make their claim to their local TEC.

The assessment consists of the review and analysis of a portfolio of evidence by an assessor (or assessors), supplemented by site visits to check out the assertions made in the portfolio and to assess within the organization its claim that it is ready for public recognition as an Investor in People.

As TEC staff, assessors and adviser-consultants continually remind colleges, the portfolio itself is used by assessors primarily to 'scope' or to design an assessment. The qualitative interviews conducted on the site visits are the real meat of the assessment. As with all auditing processes, much of the assessment is about checking systems and the documented claims and other assertions against current practice. Does the college do what it says it does? Can an assessor confirm this to his or her satisfaction? In every case, the assessor is asking if the requirements of the assessment indicators have been met.

Staff development practitioners undoubtedly have an important role to play in the assessment, too. They will certainly take a lead in supporting assessors' investigations into how the IiP principle relating to action is met and they will support the college's claims with regard to the other three principles. Yet, the college which focuses all its IiP energies on the delivery of staff development will not gain recognition. Staff development practitioners and those with overall responsibility for this function in colleges, need to recognize the limitation of their inputs and to balance these with the demands which are also made of line managers and all employees in this process.

Recognition

Assessors themselves cannot grant IiP recognition to any organization. This falls to the TEC's Recognition Panel which will meet on a regular basis to review assessors' recommendations. The TEC Recognition Panel will need to satisfy itself that the assessment has been conducted in accordance with the requirements of the assessment system. This process has now been codified and is operated on a national basis through a series of Assessment and Recognition Centres, which are quality assured by Investors in People UK.

The Recognition Panel members need to develop confidence in the assessment recommendation which has been arrived at by the assessor. Only when the panel members signify that they have such confidence will an organization be recognized as an Investor in People. As all recognized organizations know, IiP recognition is the first milepost on the journey. Inevitably, development issues will have been identified by the assessor during the assessment and communicated to the organization in the feedback interview. Thereafter, in order to sustain IiP recognition, further assessments will be made at three yearly intervals. Resulting development programmes will require continued support from line managers and staff development practitioners if they are to be successfully implemented.

Colleges and the Investors in People: notes on some specific cases

As noted above, not many colleges are ready to be recognized as Investors in People and some indication of what is happening in those embarked on the

94

journey may usefully illustrate development issues for other colleges. The following examples are all real and within the experience of the writer but some care has been taken to mask the identity of individual colleges. In various ways, the three snapshots address the vital issues of:

- the relationship between IiP and staff development;
- business management issues and their links to IiP;
- the support that IiP delivers for the ongoing development of all staff.

They indicate a series of business planning and people management issues which are reflected to a greater or lesser degree in many colleges and, indeed, in a range of other types of organization. The reasons that individual colleges are grappling with these issues are not addressed here; their situation is simply analysed with reference to progress towards IiP recognition.

College A   Finding time to sustain employee competence
This college, prior to incorporation, simply never found time for staff development activities. Workloads were heavy, there was always too much to do and staff development was characterized by 'events' which were delivered at the end of the day or at weekends or by events which failed to take place at all, given the poor projected take up of places.

The college made its public commitment to IiP in the very early days of the initiative. It was seen as a good thing by the college management team because they saw their role as part of the people development industry; they felt this was an award which the college really ought to have.

The task of gaining the award was given without consultation to the staff development manager and a timetable of approximately one year was allocated. After these decisions had been made, IiP appeared on senior management team agendas as a 'job in progress' issue only. The staff development manager, who is not a member of that team, makes termly progress reports to one gathering of the group.

To date, the college has not achieved IiP. The skill base of the staff is ossifying since the only staff development activities to be addressed are those associated with the updating of staff knowledge in established specialisms, supplemented by some interest in gaining assessor awards. Little input into reskilling and the development of newly defined skills and expertise has been made. A wholesale redundancy and early retirement programme is under way. Although the college intends to 'do something' about IiP in the near future, this will have to wait at least for now because there is so much bad feeling towards the senior management team as a result of the redundancies.

Staff development has not been embedded into the normal working life of the staff and hence the lesson that continuous development is an economic imperative in an ever changing employment world has not been recognized. The staff development manager is, at present, concentrating on getting as many lecturing staff as possible qualified as assessors of National Vocational Qualifications in order to meet awarding body requirements for assessment.

College B   Business development and effective people management
This is a college which, by its own admission, is not ready to be recognized as an Investor in People. It has identified a three year development programme in order to achieve that recognition.

This inner city college grasped the initiative as a tool for its salvation. With falling rolls, demoralized staff and the prospect of many curriculum areas simply disappearing from the timetable (for reasons associated with their lack of viability) the senior management team took the principles of IiP to the heart of its managerial activities.

This college, too, has been forced to address redundancies and early retirement as means of reducing running costs. It has identified areas into which it will channel its resources and identified which services it will offer or develop. Many programmes which its lecturing staff would have wished to sustain have gone, and new philosophies underscore the direction college development is taking.

The IiP programme is led by the Vice Principal who has already dovetailed the IiP action plan with the college's development and strategic plans, stemming from its FEFC inspection.

IiP is visible in the college; staff know that the organization has made a commitment to work towards the award. Also visible is the development process which underpins it. However, the college has indicated that two major issues need to be addressed before it can begin to speak regularly about its progress to a larger audience. One issue deals with directed staff development. The senior team is committed to the involvement of all new staff in carefully constructed induction programmes and to the involvement of all staff in staff development activities dealing with the new directions in which the college is proceeding. Attendance at both programmes is mandatory. The second issue deals with the definition of a clear human resources plan which will support the business and strategic planning activities of the college. All issues, ranging from human resource planning, recruitment and selection, induction, training and development to the termination of employment, (both voluntary and involuntary), as well as employee welfare and pensions will be addressed through this plan.

It is not as yet clear whether the radical changes which have taken place will ensure the college's survival, but the senior management team believes the college is now better placed to be in existence in two years' time than it was a year ago. In terms of progress towards IiP recognition, achievements are being made with the clear definition in business terms of the contribution of people to the success of a changing college and the embedding of focused and relevant staff development into the working day.

College C   New horizons for staff development?
This is a college situated in the high-tech hinterland of a conurbation. The college has always been enthusiastic about staff development and has, for a

number of years, been in a position to log many, many training hours in the annual analysis of staff development activity. In fact, it was the staff development manager who originally urged the senior management team to seek recognition as an Investor in People.

This manager has become the IiP 'champion' and the focus of all IiP development activity. A team which comprises representatives from the faculties meets on a monthly basis to review progress. No senior manager in the college attends this meeting regularly, although the Vice Principal (whose brief includes the human resources function) wishes to give support to the work of the team.

Difficulties have been experienced with selling the benefits of IiP to the college as a whole, although the staff development manager has run a number of sessions on this. Staff development is endorsed as a good thing, but there really is insufficient time, according to the managers, to do the things that are necessary for IiP recognition without getting involved in what can only be seen as yet more activities.

The staff development manager, a middle manager in the college, is having difficulty with two major areas of the IiP journey. In this college there is no system for evaluating performance against objectives, or of assessing whether an individual's skills are really those which are needed by the college, because the college has not, as yet, focused sufficiently on defining its skill needs. An appraisal system based on a professional development model has been running for a little over two years and, on the whole, it has been well received. The developmental process it supports is endorsed and there are difficulties associated with changing this to encompass a range of performance management issues.

Additionally, the staff development manager is having difficulty in evaluating the contribution of staff development with reference to the success of the college, and they are really struggling with the fourth IiP principle, namely evaluation. That manager has been unable to link staff development activity directly with the strategic concerns of the college and cannot, in the absence of a clear guide on the skill needs of the college, demonstrate that the staff development activities which take place are really delivering the return on investment which the assessment indicators (under the evaluation principle) require.

Since so many of the activities to be completed are those which involve major organizational change and development, the staff development practitioner can supply expert guidance and support, but they cannot effect such significant change alone and unsupported.

Some progress has been made with the IiP portfolio.

Conclusions

The messages surrounding IiP remain clear and unequivocal. Using it as a quality standard to aim for supports quality development, continuous improvement, the growth of business success and all aspects of professional development. Colleges will benefit from working towards recognition and the effort taken to achieve that recognition is worthwhile. Organizational development is never easy, but the changes which the IiP processes and implementation programmes force upon committed organizations and their functional managers (including those with responsibility for human resources and staff development), are those which will help colleges to survive, profit, grow and deliver value for money to all their customers.

The IiP initiative is also a welcome support for every employee in a college since the imperatives surrounding its implementation require all employees to sustain and develop their skills in order to maintain their employability. Without such activity, they would not be able to support their employers' business objectives, nor would they be in a position to claim to be competent practitioners in a discipline or in a function.

However, the scope of the task should not be underestimated. Organizational change is neither easy nor speedy to effect and, as the examples drawn from the experiences of real colleges indicate, the timetables for achieving the national standard must be realistic. Colleges need to proceed with their IiP programmes understanding precisely what they are setting about and to remember the experiences gained when attempting to drive forward other organizational changes. Such changes can only be effected when the people at the top give their active support.

Finally, one of the strengths of the further education sector has always been its willingness to share its successes with fellow practitioners. Therefore, colleges aspiring to meet the national standard are urged to learn how recognition has been gained by those colleges which already have it. Staff development, in particular, will be enhanced by such collaborative activities.

9 Staff appraisal and staff development in the corporate college

Derek Betts

Introduction

A number of national policy changes over the past four years may now, with hindsight, be seen to have had a significant impact on college appraisal and staff development schemes. This chapter identifies these changes and seeks to assess their effects through an analysis of the published FEFC Inspection Reports 1994/95 and from information obtained from a sample of FE colleges.

Three key policy changes head the list
First, the 1991 national salary settlement arrived at in the National Joint Council (for FE), provided for, inter alia, a framework for local negotiations on staff development, training and appraisal (NATFHE, 1991). Effect was given to this part of the agreement by the incorporation of a new paragraph (28) in the Silver Book of terms and conditions of service for further education lecturers. This states that:

> All full time staff and all part time staff on proportional contracts are required to participate in a local scheme for staff appraisal. Such schemes shall conform to the national framework agreement unless there is a joint agreement between the LEA and the recognized lecturers' union locally to depart from it.

The second major change was the fundamental one brought about by the Further and Higher Education Act of 1992 which removed the LEA from the above agreement, almost before the ink had dried, by establishing the FE Corporations. The Act also introduced the Further Education Funding Councils (FEFC), the devisors of the current funding methodology which is exerting such a powerful, and somewhat over-burdening, influence on college budgets.

It is worth noting in the context of this chapter, that this funding methodology was designed to reduce the historically wide band of colleges' unit costs inherited from the LEAs (from under £2000 per FTE student to about £5000) to a much narrower band. This objective of rapid convergence is being pursued alongside a second imperative – to increase the student enrolments by an additional 25% over a three year period. Although this policy has now been modified to a 28% increase over four years (ending in 1997), many colleges have failed to secure their second year targets, thereby adding to their financial plight. It is difficult to see how some colleges are going to escape the 'double whammy' effect of a cost cutting, demand led methodology without resorting to substantial cutbacks in expenditure.

To complete this part of the picture, it should be said that the National Association of Teachers in Further and Higher Education (NATFHE), the main lecturers' union, has been in dispute since the middle of 1993 with the Colleges' Employers Forum (CEF) over changes it has sought to make to the Silver Book contract. It is likely that this protracted dispute will have a detrimental effect on the running of appraisal schemes.

It may therefore be something of an understatement to say that the FHE Act (1992) and the dispute produced a difficult climate for appraisal schemes and staff development activities to flourish. In fact, depending on the amount of progress made in local negotiations, Paragraph 28 may not have transferred to the new corporations. However, as will be seen later, the national framework appears to have been used as the basis of college schemes irrespective of the status of the local collective agreement.

The third key change, which came about as a consequence of the second one, was the ending of the specific funding regime, the Grant for Educational Support and Training (GEST). In the last year of this earmarked staff development fund, £20m was made available to FE. When the GEST money was subsumed into the FEFC's annual budget (if, indeed, it was), it represented roughly 0.95% of the 1993/94 national allocation to colleges. This, albeit crude, calculation provides a benchmark which will be used later to compare current levels of college expenditure on staff development.

This brief, scene setting, introduction is completed by a reminder of the elements of the 1991 national appraisal scheme. This will provide another useful benchmark against which the present state of development in colleges may be judged.

The National Appraisal Scheme framework (summary)
1   The objectives and outcomes are focused on the professional development of academic staff. Other procedures exist to deal with probation, promotion, disciplinary issues and questions relating to competence. The procedure for handling appraisal should be separate from these.

100

2 The activity designated as appraisal is broader than individual lecturer appraisal. Equally important, is institutional and departmental review which should provide the context for individual appraisal.
3 Appraisal should be used positively to promote equality of opportunity.
4 All participating staff should be given access to training.
5 Appraisers must be able to engage with appraisees in a joint process of professional review and must be in a position to ensure that agreed outcomes are duly processed.
6 The process will include:
  (a) A standard appraisal cycle length, which will normally be two years but may be shorter.
  (b) An initial meeting between appraiser and appraisee to agree the purpose, focus and stages to be gone through.
  (c) Completion by the appraisee of a locally standardized self-appraisal exercise.
  (d) An evaluation of the individual's activities and effectiveness in the facilitation of learning and other activities.
  (e) The collection of data relating to the appraisee.
  (f) Preparation by the appraiser, including reflection on the relevant documentation.
  (g) The appraisal discussion.
  (h) The preparation of an agreed record focusing on objectives and outcomes for the forthcoming period.
7 A copy of the agreed full record of the appraisal discussion will be held in the confidential personnel record file.
8 Outcomes will include a set of objectives (targets or action points) and a range of recommendations in respect of staff development activities.
9 Arrangements for the monitoring and regular evaluation of the scheme shall be established.
10 There should be a procedure for hearing any complaint.
11 Colleges are to be encouraged to consider how and over what time scale hourly paid lecturers might be included in the scheme.

Analysis of the FEFC inspection reports

The most comprehensive national check on the progress that has been made in colleges since 1991 can be obtained from the series of FEFC inspection reports on individual colleges. In July 1994, the first FEFC Annual Report covering the first 60 FE colleges inspected, summarized the position on appraisal thus:

> Staff appraisal systems are being developed in most colleges, although the pace of development is slow. Appraisal is rarely linked to pay. In a

few institutions, progress on introducing appraisal has been impeded by industrial disputes about contracts of employment. (FEFC, 1994, b, p.30)

This, as it stands, does not tell us very much about the appraisal system, save the reference to the speed (or to the lack of speed) of its introduction and an observation concerning an apparent missing link with pay. If the guidelines as set down in 1991 were being followed closely, there would not be such a link in the making. So, while this aspect appears to have come as a disappointment to the FEFC inspectorate, it comes as no surprise to this observer. Nor, unfortunately, does it come as any surprise that the industrial action, referred to earlier, may have had a detrimental effect on developments in this area of college activity.

Reducing the text of the 60 college reports to a three sentence annual summary is bound to leave much to the imagination. However, by studying the present collection of 105 college reports (and recognizing that there is now a time difference of approximately 18 months between the early and later reports), it is possible to represent a much fuller picture of appraisal schemes than was possible in the FEFC's Annual Report.

Using the eleven point national appraisal framework as a template, and classifying the inspectors' comments that were made on the 105 colleges, the following table can be constructed showing some of the strengths and weaknesses that were highlighted.

Table 1: Incidence of elements from the 11-point national appraisal framework which appear in the 105 FEFC Inspection Reports, 1994–95

Element	Description		No of times occurring
1	Distinct appraisal procedures		0
2	Appraisal as part of broader review		0
3	Promotion of equal opportunities		0
4	Access to training appraisers/appraisees		21
5	Identity of appraisers (line managers)		6
6	Process	(a) length of cycle 2 years	8
		(b) length of cycle 1 year	5
7	Confidential records		2
8	Link	with staff development	43
		with college strategic plans	15
9	Monitoring/evaluation arrangements		11
10	Complaints procedure		2
11	Part time staff involvement		0

The absence of many references to the full range of elements from the national framework is probably explained by the impression given in the reports that the inspectors' first priority was to record the stage reached in the development of schemes without being overly concerned about some of the detail.

Hence, of the 105 colleges inspected

11	had no appraisal scheme in place,
17	were at the pilot stage,
36	were part way through the first round,
41	had completed at least one full cycle.

These figures suggest that the lack of pace in the development of appraisal schemes, as observed in the first 60 colleges inspected, may not be an accurate reflection of the present position. With the additional 45 college reports now to hand and the corresponding passage of time, the pace does seem to have quickened.

As Table 1 shows, the inspectors' attention was also drawn to evidence of training for appraisal schemes and to the frequently mentioned links they make with staff development activities. They also noted that some schemes involved classroom observation (in 14 reports), and produced teacher satisfaction (in 15 reports).

This rather fragmentary information is likely to reflect more the various inspectors' perception of the main features than to provide evidence for thinking that the national framework is not being used as the basis for local schemes. Later on, we can look at some first hand evidence from colleges to see if the shape of the intended model is still intact.

Before leaving the FEFC reports, there are several items of quantitative information, directly related to staff appraisal and staff development, which may well help to explain the pace of, and variations in, progress. The areas concerned are: (a) the size of the staff development budgets, (b) the extent of colleges' involvement with the Investors in People award, and (c) changing balance between part time and full time posts.

(a) Funding

Bearing in mind the GEST funding benchmark quoted earlier, there is an interesting passage from the John Baillie Memorial Lecture given by Ruth Gee, Chief Executive of the Association for Colleges. In it, she quotes some research carried out for the AfC by the Institute of Education on the question of GEST and the current funding levels (Young et al., 1994):

> Changes in GEST, and the fact that FEFC does not explicitly allocate funds for professional development, increases the pressure to provide short term INSET programmes, rather than meet long term planning requirements. The Institute of Education research shows that, in the London area alone, practice is varied. Some colleges insist that all new staff are trained, others have no policy. A teaching qualification is encouraged, but never required, for part time staff. Expenditure on

staff development varies between 1.5% and 4%, of which the majority appears to go on G/NVQ assessor training and management training. I suspect that a national survey would show a wider spectrum of practice, especially at the lower end. (Gee, 1994, p.20)

Ruth Gee's instincts about the likely results from a national survey are correct if the information given in the 105 FEFC reports represents accurately the wider national picture. In 50 reports, the level of funding on staff development was identifiable and has been, in all cases, converted to a percentage of the college budget. This was necessary because a number of the reports related the percentage to the staffing budget. The FEFC figures exhibit the following characteristics:

1　The average level of funding is 1.09%
2　The modal level of funding is 1.00%
3　The range is from 0.33% to 3.00%

Within the range, 21 colleges were below, and 18 colleges were above the 11 colleges whose funding for staff development was reported at 1%. Even if all the figures from the Institute of Education's survey had been measured against the respective staffing budgets, the FEFC returns support Ruth Gee's view that there is, indeed, a wider spectrum of practice, especially at the lower end. If this sample of colleges is, in any way, representative of all FE colleges, it would mean that 40% of them were operating staff development budgets below the former GEST level.

(b) Investors in People (IiP)

The pattern of colleges' increasing involvement in IiP, the Employment Department's initiative which seeks to link staff training to company objectives, can be seen in the following statistics:

No. of colleges not involved	36	(34.3%)
No. of colleges working towards award	29	(27.6%)
No. of colleges with a 1995 target	21	(20.5%)
No. of colleges with a 1996 target	9	(8.6%)
No. of colleges with an IiP award	10	(9.0%)
	105	

There appears to be a broad congruence between this pattern and the earlier one which described the stages colleges had reached in developing staff appraisal schemes. That is, a third are at the starting gate, (or worse), a third are in mid-race, and a third are in sight of the winning post, (or better). Since the IiP initiative places staff training and employee competence at the centre of an organization's concerns, the only surprise would have been if the patterns had been quite different.

(c) Part time/full time staffing ratios

This may not, at first sight, appear to be very relevant to this analysis. However, for a variety of reasons which are often connected with resources, part time hourly paid staff are less likely to be included in appraisal and staff development schemes. In fact, the majority are excluded.

Figures from the FEFC reports show that, on average, the part time proportion of the total full time equivalent staff is 28%. (A recent wider survey by Education Lecturing Services (ELS) estimated a 30% ratio). The variations from the FEFC returns put the range of the part time proportion at 9% to 52%. [Note: Part time staff include proportional staff as well as hourly paid.]

Anecdotal evidence certainly suggests that the percentage of part-timers is growing. The college with 52% may be the exception at the moment, but there were seven colleges in the survey with ratios over 40%. The implication for future staff appraisal and staff development programmes, as far as part time staff are concerned, must be one of increasing difficulty. If colleges are unable to offer part time staff much access to programmes now, the situation cannot be improved by an increase in part time staff numbers.

Pen pictures of local appraisal schemes in action

While the FEFC reports revealed a lot of useful information of a broad brush kind, something of the detail is inevitably lost in journey from data collection to edited report. Glimpses of the nationally agreed appraisal framework were seen but how closely do college schemes mirror the guidelines that were set in 1991?

To try to find out, the same 11 point appraisal scheme used in Table 1 earlier was discussed with seven colleges where staff appraisal schemes are being pursued actively. The college identities are hidden behind the letters of the alphabet.

Individual staff appraisal schemes: interview responses

1 *Are the appraisal procedures distinct from other procedures (e.g. promotion)?*
A They have been kept separate by the managers in their appraisal interviews. However, it is difficult for staff, particularly those whose relationship with their line manager is not of the best, to perceive that the two really are separate.
   We do not appraise staff in their probationary year. We run a support/ mentor scheme which includes classroom visits.
B The current scheme predates the NJC agreement by five years. Two principles have guided its introduction and operation: the involvement of staff at all stages and a demonstrable commitment.
   The various procedures are theoretically distinct but, in practice, there can be a blurring at the edges by overlapping usage. While any probation period is certainly excluded from appraisal, individual staff members may wish to

refer to appraisal reports as evidence to be used in either promotion interviews or disciplinary hearings.

C Probation is excluded and it is intended that other procedures should remain separate. In reality there may be a bit of blurring.

D Not linked in any way. If there is any overlap it would be the fault of the appraisee/appraiser.

E There is some blurring in practice.

F The various procedures are kept separate. No use of reports is permitted outside the appraisal process. Probation is excluded from the process and there is no promotion policy.

G The procedures are kept separate; the only variation occurs where staff may authorize the use of their reports for the purpose of constructing references.

2 *Is appraisal part of a broader review?*

A Individual lecturer appraisal feeds into faculty review which, in turn, informs the annual institutional review. Issues relating to resources go to advisory meetings at faculty level, issues of training to the staff development team, issues of communication to the VP and Deans working group.

B Institutional and sectoral aims are included in the scheme.

C Sectoral issues are considered to some extent, but not consistently. Staff development is focused towards the individual's needs.

D A bit weak on this point. We are beginning to get there. IiP has helped in this process. Position papers from each sector are considered as part of strategic planning and the quality assurance scheme has generated some flows of information.

E There is a system of course review and strategic planning.

F Keen on the principle which has not yet been fully implemented. There is a system of self-evaluation as part of the appraisal process and team appraisal is being promoted (but not fully developed). Review at faculty level is lacking and at institutional level it is flimsy.

G The 'blueprint' is in place but the system is not yet being applied universally. A lack of management skills is at the root of the problem.

3 *Is appraisal making a positive contribution to promoting equal opportunities?*

A The training for appraisal stressed that this was crucial. In as much as everyone is appraised according to the same system I suppose it helps EO, in as much as managers are better informed about their staff's capabilities and aspirations, it ought to, but... what would be the criteria to show that it actually does have a *direct* relationship?

B Appraisal should be used in this way but I am not wholly convinced that it does. Line managers (who are appraisers) are mostly men. Different approaches would seem to be needed.

C Appraisal is linked to the college's equal opportunity policy.

D It is an aim of the policy. There is a continuous improvement group for appraisal where review can take place.

E Our policies are separate but complementary.

F One policy promotes the other. EO policy is a priority. Appraisees may nominate anyone (trained) but there is no peer group appraisal.

G Yes, in theory, but how do you achieve a positive outcome? There is a need to keep the appraisal scheme in line with the college's overall equal opportunities policy.

4 Is there access to training for appraisers/appraisees?

A Yes.

B All staff have been trained. Six sessions, covering all aspects of the procedure, are provided annually in which appraisers and appraisees are trained together. (Appraisees may become appraisers and, in any case, each group needs to understand the others' perspective.)

C Yes.

D Yes, this is an IiP commitment. Training is carried out jointly, as it should be.

E Yes, jointly. 50/60% take up, and there is an advanced programme available, as well.

F Yes, all invited and all attend. Some distinct training for appraisers is provided.

G We trained everybody together in the first round. Now we are training the two groups separately. The appraisers did not feel confident. We have also developed an advanced programme which is compulsory for appraisers and optional for appraisees.

5 Who are the appraisers?

A Line managers in this institution are not responsible for staff. So the Heads of School appraise in one year of two, and the Deans (the real line managers in charge of staff), do so in the following year. HoS observe a classroom session for all teaching staff. Latter can be carried out by staff development team if staff member is unhappy about line manager (HoS) doing it. Can ask for VP(HRD) instead of Dean but not encouraged to do so. [SD team has done classroom appraisal in schools where HoS is not teacher trained]. All classroom appraisers must be teacher trained.

B Line managers and section leaders. Staff have some choice in so far as each may exercise up to two rejections before an appraiser is assigned.

C Line manager or by peer group assessment. Appraisal by line manager could be artificial because of the day-to-day working relationship. Appraisees have a choice through negative preference.

D The first line manager (and up the line, if necessary). No choice for the individual.

E The first line manager. There is a monitoring group which carries out reviews by questionnaire. Any problems with the appraiser/appraisee relationship can be identified and rectified.

F There are criteria for the choice of appraiser. Knowledge of the area of work and of the job, together with mutual trust and confidence. Normally, the first line manager is chosen.

G The criteria used are:
• familiarity with the area of work
• trained
• power to deploy the necessary resources
Normally, first line managers (but it is possible to 'go up the line' after any problems are talked through). A choice of non-line managers is possible where cross-college jobs are involved.

6 *Do the following processes describe the scheme?*
   (a) A standard appraisal cycle length, which will normally be two years but may be shorter.
   (b) An initial meeting between appraiser and appraisee to agree the purpose, focus and stages to be gone through.
   (c) Completion by the appraisee of a locally standardized self-appraisal exercise.
   (d) An evaluation of the individual's activities and effectiveness in the facilitation of learning and other activities.
   (e) The collection of data relating to the appraisee.
   (f) Preparation by the appraiser, including reflection on the relevant documentation.
   (g) The appraisal discussion.
   (h) The preparation of an agreed record focusing on objectives and outcomes for the forthcoming period.

A Yes.

B Yes, the only amendment is to the length of the appraisal cycle which is now annual (on staff insistence!)

C Yes, the only changes are:
(d) Discussion, not evaluation.
(e) By negotiation.
(h) Followed by a six month review.
There is pressure from staff for an annual review, and pressure from appraisers for a 3-year one on the grounds of a lack of resources.

D Yes, with the following modifications:
(d) Discussion, not evaluation.
(h) Two forms, one interview form to one line manager up the line, one staff development form to staff development officer.
Sometimes it has been possible to provide an annual review (but resources prevent this being applied generally.)

E Yes, with the following changes:
(a) Annually.
(d) Discussion, not evaluation.
(h) Two sheets: one to staff development plan, one to personnel records. Monitoring group keep a continuous professional development plan up-to-date through a questionnaire process.
F Yes.
G Reduced the cycle to an annual one.
All stages are applied to new staff but (b) is not used for existing staff. For them, the annual interview is subdivided into a review session (which is logged) followed by a forward planning session. Classroom observation is used where relevant. The underlying principle is to be creative.

7 *Is the custody of reports in confidential personnel files?*
A Yes.
B Yes, with a copy to individual.
C Yes, and record of meeting to appraisee/appraiser and record of outcomes to staff development team.
D Yes.
E Yes (as C above).
F Yes.
G Yes.

8 *Is there a link with staff development and a delivery of outcomes thereafter?*
A Sore point. Our union branch is blocking the appraisal scheme as part of the dispute over new contracts. It agrees with our system, but is withholding cooperation with it as a 'weapon' against management. Of five faculties, 60% of three are taking part and about 10% of the other two.
Outcomes are fed to the staff development team to incorporate into general programmes or targeted activities for the individual.
B Yes, there is a link and all staff have been appraised. Individuals often seek to modify their action plans after the agreed record is made (in the light of further experience and on second thoughts, etc.).
There is a formal review as well.
C There is a link and delivery is getting better, not perfect yet. 50% of staff have been appraised so far.
D Only 30 staff have been appraised so far, so the delivery side cannot properly be assessed yet. Position papers are published by each sector to encourage individuals to see their place in the overall strategy.
E Staff development is tied into the appraisal scheme. Questionnaires will be handled by the monitoring group which has just been formed to ensure the delivery of outcomes.

F Some staff think that it is purposeful but there are problems and a danger of 'going through the motions' if not solved. 80% of staff have been appraised.

G The links are in place to deliver staff development. Some staff still focus on long courses as the appropriate (the only?) form of staff development which has value.

80% of staff have been appraised.

9 Are there effective monitoring/evaluation arrangements in place?

A Working group is in place to review the operation of the system but not yet operative because of the industrial action.

Staff tutor who carried out training is carrying out a programme of follow up evaluation visits to the appraisers to collect feedback on the effectiveness of the training as a preparation for their role.

B Evaluation is through a formal two year review. Monitoring is on the basis of anonymous case studies (which has resulted in the barring of two people from the cohort of appraisers as unsuitable for the process).

C Monitoring is by a six month review. Evaluation is being considered – not in place.

D Monitoring and evaluation is handled by the Continuous Improvement Group.

E At the moment, monitoring is through a questionnaire but the monitoring group is to pilot a more comprehensive system to include evaluation.

F In the main, monitoring/evaluation is poor. This comes out in the IiP documentation. Insufficient linkage between staff development and business objectives.

G Through a process of questionnaires with a full annual review.

10 Is there an agreed complaints procedure?

A Yes.

B Individual formal review process generally picks up the little problems but an agreed procedure is available.

C Yes.

D Informally, but if it fails, the grievance procedure can be used.

E Yes.

F Informally.

G Yes.

11 To what extent are hourly paid lecturers included in staff appraisal/staff development?

A When a Dean/HoS feels that the person's contribution is sufficiently substantial to warrant it, and if that person wishes to be involved. Not routinely.

B Staff appraisal for all substantial part-timers (over eight hours), for others it is optional.

110

Staff development is available for all part-timers. Cannot afford payment, though.

C Open to all substantial part-timers (who receive half pay).

D All part-timers receive a one-hour induction and a one-hour annual review as part of their contract. The annual review takes the form of self-appraisal and/or a joint discussion with the section.

E Too expensive to consider appraisal for part-timers (we use a self-assessment form). Staff development is offered at £10 per hour.

F Would love to! Only substantive part-timers are invited (if possible).

G Part-timers are offered support. No takers, so far.

12 Does your college hold an IiP award?

A Not yet – we are well on the way but put it on hold during the strikes over contracts. (Inspection has just been completed)

B We have had the award for some time. Useful to do it once to secure external confirmation of good practice. Revalidation will be an issue. (Is the continued use of the logo worth the additional cost?)

C Contemplating an application.

D Working towards one.

E Working towards one. It is a useful framework for judging good practice.

F Working towards one (slowly).

G We have the IiP award.

13 What is the size of your staff development budget?

A 1%

B 1%

C 1% and struggling

D 1%

E 1.5%

F 1% and struggling to maintain it.

G 1.5%

These findings are in line with those of the FEFC inspectors but have the air of greater authenticity which comes from bypassing the sieve of the edited report. More importantly, they confirm that the 1991 national guidelines have been followed locally in large measure. The adaptations made to the appraisal process (Qu. 6) demonstrate sensible working arrangements which might even point to an initially conservative approach having been taken in 1991.

These findings also show the same spread of involvement with IiP and the same average 1% for staff development budgets as was found in the FEFC reports. This suggests that these experiences are in the mainstream of developments and might, therefore, provide a useful yardstick.

It is very important to remember here that many serious criticisms were made by the inspectors about some aspects of college schemes and there is some self-criticism inherent in the pen pictures. Staff satisfaction of appraisal schemes was identified in 16% of FEFC college reports. It would be interesting to know how the other 84% of staff feel but difficult to measure in a comprehensive way.

Since a healthy level of staff support for appraisal schemes is a prerequisite for their success, it would be useful to have an accurate assessment of staff attitudes in the current conditions. The long running industrial action, referred to earlier, is a distorting factor. It has distracted attention away from many issues. The evidence uncovered in this analysis is fragmentary. There is evidence of staff satisfaction, of staff dissatisfaction and union action in blocking some developments. The dynamics of this situation may well change (one way or the other) whenever the national dispute over new contracts is finally ended. After that, staff will inevitably turn their attention to some of the issues that are raised in the concluding paragraphs.

Conclusions

Perhaps this is the moment to adopt a more personal style in trying to make some sense of the information that has been gathered in. I think a good starting point for this exercise would be to look again at three 'official' conclusions drawn by the FEFC's Inspectorate in the 1994 Annual Report (FEFC, 1994).

Their conclusions on staff appraisal developments were quoted on pp.101–102. These did not attempt to reveal much detail about the emerging schemes although we have now seen that there are many negative and positive aspects that could be balanced in a debate about good practice.

As far as complementary staff development schemes are concerned, the FEFC found much more to enthuse about although I felt that the original reports were generally rather bland in comparison. Their conclusions focused on:
* the high priority given to staff development
* linkages with strategic objectives
* moves to IiP status
* variability of resources devoted to staff development
* predominance of TDLB programmes.

I would suggest that Ruth Gee's summary (which appears on pp.103–104), gets much closer to the sense that prevails in colleges at the moment. The modest level and variability of funding does not suggest that staff development is being given a very high priority. Short term measures are getting preference over those that would meet longer term planning requirements.

Finally, the FEFC's college ratings, which are applied to broad areas of college activity, put quality assurance (which includes staff appraisal/staff development) at the bottom of the averaged scores for the year. On the scale 1 (strong) to

5 (weak), averaging the grades awarded to the 60 colleges in 1994 produced the following results:

		Average Score
1	Responsiveness and Range of Provision	1.87
2	Resources	2.05
3	Student Recruitment, Guidance and Support	2.19
4	Governance and Management	2.39
5	Quality Assurance	2.61

If these figures mean anything, then one must assume that the inspectors have more concerns about quality assurance procedures than about the other four areas of activity.

The period 1991 to 1995 has seen more progress made in the area of staff development than could have been predicted in 1990. What then seemed to be generally lacking, was a systematic approach to needs analysis and a trustworthy mechanism for ensuring the achievement of any objectives that might be set. Whatever might now be the status of paragraph 28 of the Silver Book regarding the appraisal framework, the national collective agreement seems to be maintaining an influence on local developments.

Evidence has been given in the pen-pictures which indicates that every element of the framework has been addressed and amended where necessary to produce a workable scheme. Perhaps there is a lesson here about the full involvement of staff (nationally and locally) at all developmental stages of an initiative, even at the cost of a longer time scale than some would desire. Decision makers too often seem to regard the connected systems of prior consultation, genuine pilots and independent evaluation as time consuming nuisances.

The parallel introduction of the Investors in People award (seen by many as a more acceptable initiative than a plethora of unwanted ones such as glossy Charters for the Citizen) seems to have helped in supporting the development of appraisal schemes. Certainly, all the feedback suggests that colleges have committed themselves more readily to IiP than to, say, BS5750. Two prominent and tangible benefits of IiP are the use of a 'template' through which to check internal procedures and the value of an independent external adviser who can confirm the validity of the college's approach.

A logo comes with it, of course, but interestingly, one college sees its acquisition as of secondary importance. So much so, that the college is now assessing the *value* of continuing to use the logo against the continuing *cost* of maintaining it.

According to the analysis of the FEFC inspection reports, less than 10% of colleges have reached the IiP award stage. All may however, be encouraged to consider the findings that arise from this analysis.

Reflections on the future

There are five main areas in the analysis where specific conclusions can be drawn and which may, in turn, reflect on good practice, or perhaps better practice.

1   The 1991 national appraisal framework was a collective agreement. In turn, local collective agreements have to involve the staff at all stages up to the point of final agreement when both 'sides' actually own the outcomes. Staff satisfaction (as observed by the FEFC) cannot be achieved by imposition, a lesson that might have been learned from the imposition of TDLB programmes.

2   Funding levels are not very high and are clearly very variable. Given the present climate, there is little prospect of a reversal of the downward spiral of unit costs. In this situation, staff development budgets will remain vulnerable to cutbacks. There are just too many people willing the ends and too few willing the means. And there is an irony in relation to the GEST funding. The government introduced the specific grant system when it believed that LEAs were providing low and variable levels of staff development funding. We are back to low and variable levels but now associated with the application of market forces. No college should be setting a staff development budget which falls below the old GEST levels.

3   Notwithstanding the financial constraints, the pen pictures showed that a number of changes and additions can be made to the appraisal framework within the spirit of the national guidelines. These could be construed as examples of good practice.

I would draw particular attention to the following points:

•   An annual appraisal rather than 2-year cycles.
    The 2-year cycle was originally chosen with a concern about resources in mind. The subsequent lack of progress in developing and applying schemes of appraisal in some colleges has certainly been linked to the resource issue. It is equally clear, however, that pressure from the staff in some colleges has resulted in the adoption of annual appraisals.

•   The different but tangible links to staff development.
    Establishing this link was a crucial element of the 1991 agreement. In the joint commentary to the agreement, it was suggested that 'as improvement of quality is the primary objective, [it] was essential to concentrate upon the professional development of academic staff who are the central resource in the system'. (NATFHE, 1991, p.10)

•   The emerging review, monitoring and evaluation procedures.
    These procedures are gradually being applied to the appraisal process itself and, while it may be early days, some modifications are being made to the college schemes.

- **The use of 'discussion', not 'evaluation'**
  It was felt by those who made this change that the word 'discussion' conveyed the intention of the 1991 agreement as represented by another extract from the joint commentary:

  > Appraisal provides a means by which individual members of staff, in conjunction with a trained appraiser can review their skills, experiences, strengths and weaknesses and their current responsibilities and role within the college and identify ways in which the two might more effectively be combined to improve delivery. (NATFHE, 1991, p.10)

  This approach is underpinned by a quote from an ACAS publication on Employee Appraisal: 'The appraisal interview is likely to be more constructive when pay is not part of the *discussion* ... [it] is likely to obscure a genuine *discussion* both of achievements and of areas where improvement is necessary'. (ACAS, 1988 , p.30, my emphasis)
- **The various ways of choosing appraisers.**
  While most schemes followed the national advice about involving line managers, there were a number of examples where alternative appraisers could be selected. The widening of choice occurred in some institutions as a direct result of the monitoring process.

4   The burgeoning of part time staff numbers will pose increasing problems. Readers may wish to ponder the marketing blandishments of the infant Education Lecturing Services. This new employment agency for part time (to be deemed self-employed) lecturers aims to have a data base able to hold 400,000 names. Each lecturer, it is claimed, will be supported by the establishment of accredited training and development opportunities.

However, it looks as though colleges, not ELS, will be the vehicle for achieving this target. This is because each lecturer employed will have been subject to a quality check by ELS, presumably based on reports received from the employing colleges and written by the line managers who may also be appraisers.

New lecturers will be allowed to become members of the Agency only if they have been trained and have been assessed as being suitable. By whom? It looks as though some college staff, perhaps from the staff development team, will be given an additional responsibility if college management decides to dispense with a policy of employing their own part time lecturers.

5   Finally, we come to what could become the biggest issue of all, but I will mention it only in passing because it is dealt with elsewhere in this book. Suffice it to say, that a huge question mark currently hangs over the linked issues of TDLB standards, a possible education lead body, the role of a GTC and the involvement (or not) of the TTA in FE teacher training. What this

alphabet soup of acronyms does not yet add up to, is another set of acronyms, namely QTS (FE) plus CPD. The achievement of a coherent framework of qualifications and linked professional development has not been sought with the same vigour as is now being demonstrated in pursuit of so-called 'professional' contracts. I know which manifestation of professional recognition lecturers would prefer to have.

The above reflections on the future point to five separate debates: the role of collective action, the level of adequate funding, the further development of the appraisal/staff development processes, the training opportunities for part-timers and the structure of professional qualifications. I do not believe that the profession has the luxury of reflecting on these matters for too long before coming to some definite conclusions and being prepared to take the appropriate action.

10 Teacher as researcher: collaborative approaches and distance learning

Lorna Unwin

Introduction

Teachers in FE have been engaged in a massive pedagogical shift in recent years in order to adapt to the introduction of competence-based approaches, increased emphasis on individualized learning, greater diversity in the student population and the demands of new funding methodologies. At the same time, universities which offer Masters degrees to FE staff have themselves had to construct more flexible programmes in recognition of the changing needs and circumstances of the professionals they seek to serve. The days when teachers would travel, after work, to their nearest university for a Masters in Education (MEd) programme delivered one evening a week during conventional term times may be coming to an end. As well as the Open University, other universities are now developing Masters degrees, and, indeed, taught doctorates, to be delivered in a distance learning mode. The attractions for teachers include being able to work at their own pace, having structured reading and critical commentary available in digestible form, benefiting from the more concentrated study approaches available in residential schools and not being confined to the choices on offer at their local university. The challenge for the university lecturers involved in distance learning is how to develop meaningful relationships with both their students and their students' places of work in order to ensure professional development does not become confined to a more elaborate form of correspondence course. At its best, professional development should encourage FE teachers to see themselves as researchers engaged in critical enquiry. The flexibility and responsiveness that distance learning can provide should be built on by university departments of education and so facilitate collaborative activity in which both college and university staff share their expertise and experience.

This chapter explores the ways in which university accredited professional development, through the vehicle of distance learning, might create a new

117

dynamic for bringing together the three key stakeholders: the providing university; the FE teacher; and the FE college. In doing so, it draws on the collaborative arrangements I have established between my own department and two colleges located in other parts of the country.

Breaking out of the professional vocational-academic divide

As a lecturer in a university education department, I am in a very privileged position. Through the powers invested in my university to award higher degrees, I can put on courses for the education profession, I can supervise those who want to do research degrees, and I can carry out research (funded or non-funded) into the aspects of education which interest me. I do, of course, have certain requirements to fulfil which impinge on the relative freedom which academics enjoy. Such requirements include meeting target numbers for postgraduate students and contributing to the department's research and publications profile for the research selectivity exercise. There is, however, no specific requirement to work with, in a collaborative sense, the education profession whether at local, regional or national level. Such collaboration does, of course, exist in all university education departments, but the point I wish to make is that academics in those departments can if they wish confine their relationships with practitioners to two functions:

1 the academic takes the role of teacher of the teachers;
2 the academic takes the role of researcher of educational policy and practice.

In the first function, the academic has the whip hand in that however much the courses involved might be run in a genuinely participatory, pedagogical manner and draw heavily on the students' professional expertise and experience, it is the academic who is seen as the ultimate authority and source of knowledge. In the second function, the academic may have to tread more carefully in order to ensure access to data and people, but again the relationship is tilted in the academic's favour. Such hierarchical notions separate academic from practitioners in ways which replicate the long standing barriers between the academic and the vocational in wider society.

The single most pressing debate in post-16 education continues to be about this so-called 'academic-vocational divide' which separates children and young adults in terms of curricula, qualifications and progression opportunities. This debate has raged in countless books, articles, conference papers and policy documents. Ironically, whilst this divide is seen as a major issue for academic debate, a version of the divide could be said to exist within the very education departments which debate its existence. Hence, teachers leave their vocational context to enter an academic arena in which their vocational expertise may, but not necessarily, be credited or built upon.

118

This divide is compounded by the curious position of academic publications. Journal articles, books and other research-based material form the bedrock of professional development courses and introduce practitioners to the huge array of research and critical theory which emanates out of their professional context. Sadly, many practitioners will never read this material unless they participate in an academic course and even then, because some of the material is too impenetrable, they lose their initial interest. That impenetrability often results from the fact that many authors regard the primary audience for their material as being comprised of fellow academics rather than members of the teaching profession. This means that the dissemination of important research findings and critical commentary can be narrowly restricted and, perhaps most significantly, result in further academic theorizing rather than action to improve education policies and practices. As Kelly has argued, it is of course, important that people continue to study education from the outside, to give an 'external perspective' but:

> ...this will lead to untold dangers, ...and may even be counterproductive to educational advance, if it is not complemented by a study of education from the inside, a study focused on the realities of teachers' practice... This is something which all teachers must learn, and be helped, to do for themselves. (Kelly, 1993, pp.131–2)

In addition to the problem of academic publications remaining unread by practitioners, there is a further rich source of research-based literature whose potential is largely undervalued. That source consists of the countless dissertations and theses prepared for postgraduate degree courses, material which sits on library shelves and may be occasionally consulted by practitioners who are preparing their own project reports or, again, by the academics themselves. As anyone who is involved in professional development courses will know, one of the most rewarding outcomes occurs when practising teachers develop enough confidence to both read and challenge the research literature.

In order to ensure that educational research is widely disseminated, to encourage teachers to become researchers in their own right, and to help teachers understand and cope with the turbulence inherent in their profession, university education departments and the wider education profession have to form more collaborative ways of working together.

Action research and collaboration

Since the late 1960s and the early work of Lawrence Stenhouse, there has been interest in and development of collaborative projects which encourage teachers across the educational sectors to engage in research, particularly action research (see Elliott and Sarland, 1995). Action research has particular attractions and relevance to education because, as Somekh has pointed out:

It directly addresses the knotty problem of the persistent failure of research in the social sciences to make a difference in terms of bringing about actual improvements in practice. It does so by rejecting the concept of a two stage process in which research is carried out first by researchers and then in a separate second stage the knowledge generated from the research is applied by practitioners.(Somekh, 1995, p.340)

And, as Carr and Kemmis (1986) have argued, action research has an empowering role which not only promotes teachers as researchers but allows them to critically reflect on both that research and their work in general:

Educational action research engages, extends and transforms the self-understandings of practitioners by involving them in the research process. Far from appropriating practitioners' self-understandings and formulating them within theoretical or interpretative frameworks shaped by the concerns and interests of outside observers, action research involves practitioners directly in theorizing their own practice and revising their theories self-critically in the light of their practical consequences.(Carr and Kemmis, 1986, p.198)

Whilst, on the surface, the case for action research appears difficult to refute, there is an inherent danger to be addressed for the action research model can lead to an overly positivist approach which encourages teachers to concentrate almost solely on their practice. Avis (1993), who has written about the need to be wary of teacher researchers appropriating pseudo-scientific methodologies, summarises the dangers thus:

It is likely teacher researchers will focus on the immediate and practical issues that face them in their work. Such research will deliver an immediate pay off being amenable to practice/policy implementation. In this way a body of research is developed that is policy orientated and takes the language of problem solving. Such research can speak the 'truth' in such a way as to prioritize its own meanings and certitudes at the expense of other interpretations. This tendency is worrying for it closes off analysis and produces research strategies that are limited. (Avis, 1993, pp.200–1)

By turning away from the 'productive' model of research and calling for researchers to 'recognize our positionality... as classed, gendered, and raced subjects', Avis suggests that '...we raise the vulnerability of our practices to contestation'. From this new position, according to Avis, we can then 'debunk' the 'mythology' and 'purity' of research. (ibid.)

Certainly, the word 'research' is itself problematic. For some teachers, the word suggests a mysterious process, something complicated and time consuming which is removed from their general competence. The following comments from college lecturers, who were students on a Masters' degree course I ran in 1994, capture this sense of research as an alien business:

> Research is something really clever people do... I don't see myself as being able to do it. I'd be too worried about sample sizes and whether I could prove something and I'd worry that someone else had done the same thing and theirs was better.

> One tutor I had talked about conceptual frameworks... I couldn't really get my head round what he meant. I mean I can't just interview people can I, though I'd like to talk to my students about what their feelings are about the new assessment we brought in but that's not research is it?

There are other problems, too, to be faced in attempting to make action research the focus for a new relationship between further and higher education. Firstly, there is the practical question of how and when college staff might engage in research. Staff in colleges are faced with ever increasing workloads brought about because of the enormous changes in further education in recent years (see Young et. al., 1995). On top of this change, colleges have, since incorporation in 1993, introduced new contracts which require that far more time is spent in class contact and that lecturers be seen on the premises rather than trusted to continue their professional activities away from the college buildings. Secondly, there is the question of whether college staff have any enthusiasm left at the end of the day to explore their practice. For example, many of the curriculum changes in FE, and notably those associated with the introduction of competence-based qualifications, have resulted in a massive increase in paperwork and general bureaucracy.

Thirdly, we have to recognize that the nature of professional development and, in particular, the opportunity for further and higher education to work together, are under threat. At the time of writing, there is a strong possibility that a lead body for FE will be established to define standards for FE teachers and support staff in order to place professional qualifications within the NVQ framework. In addition, the newly formed Teacher Training Agency is pursuing a strategy which will shift more and more of the training of teachers away from university education departments into schools and colleges. As a result, several departments may become unviable, thus reducing the availability of postgraduate courses and the mechanisms for giving academic credit for action research projects.

Despite these considerable barriers to the development of action research and collaborative arrangements, there are two key reasons for optimism:

1 There is a growing interest in the concept of the college as a *learning organization*, a term borrowed from private industry and one which recognizes the need for staff within any organization to play an active part in improving its policies and practices. (See, for example, Peters and Waterman, 1982; Pedlar et. al., 1989.) Such terms as the *learning organization* can, of course, be appropriated for cynical reasons by managements whose rhetoric promotes commitment to staff development, openness and democracy but whose practices equate to a very different reality. Any organization which decides to go down this route has to be prepared for the can of worms which will almost certainly be opened in the process of consulting staff and holding policies and practices up to serious scrutiny (see Unwin, 1991).

2 It would be wrong to underestimate the desire of college staff to want to explore their professional activity. The following comments are taken from interviews with college lecturers in 1994:

> I wanted to do this MA because it offers me the chance to just sit back and think about my work, to ask some tough questions... there's so little time in the normal day to do this but the questions don't go away, they just get bottled up inside.

> Those of us at college who are doing courses find we can understand better the situation... such as the curriculum changes, why they're in a particular shape, and wider issues like why some students drop out... there are lots of parts of our work that we should discuss and if you're doing a course it gives you a sort of excuse to break out of the 'Oh, it's all a fault of management' or 'It used to be okay in FE but now it's all gone wrong' mentality.

The challenge for both university education departments and colleges is to find ways of creating opportunities for people to explore their professional activity in a realistic way, one which recognizes the demands of their working lives.

Distance learning: its possibilities and limitations

As I noted in the introduction to this chapter, many universities are introducing distance learning courses at postgraduate level. To most people, the term 'distance learning' is synonymous with the Open University whose students study from prepared multimedia materials supplemented by support from locally-based tutors and residential periods at summer schools. The definition of 'distance learning' is, however, becoming much more fluid as people are prepared to travel considerable distances to participate in a course of their choice or, in the case of research degree students, to visit their supervisor. It can be a tortuous process if one becomes too embroiled in definitions but it is necessary to point out here that I have used the term 'distance learning' deliberately, as opposed to using the more ambiguous terms 'flexible learning' or 'open learning'. By focusing on 'distance learning', I want to highlight the fact that relationships between further and higher education institutions now transcend the physical difficulties imposed by distance and that the central features of well planned and supported distance learning can provide a useful framework for promoting action research and the concept of the teacher as researcher.

In order to facilitate attendance, some education departments have restructured their courses around residential weekend study with students following structured reading programmes (rather than the traditional packaged distance learning materials) in between the weekends. This allows departments to recruit students nationally. For the students, having to attend a certain number of residential weekends, during say a two year Masters programme, gives them a welcome opportunity to escape from domestic duties, concentrate their minds on their studies and spend more time with their tutors. Perhaps most importantly, it also provides a congenial atmosphere in which to share ideas with fellow professionals from other colleges at a time when institutions are becoming more and more insular as a result of having to operate in the competitive marketplace which has arisen since incorporation. Where once college staff may have met at events organized by LEAs, they now have few opportunities to converse with colleagues outside their own institutions.

The growth of distance learning is not, however, trouble free for it is a mode of learning which can allow poor educational practice to go unchecked and leave the student isolated and without adequate tutorial support. It can be seen as cheap way to deliver courses and in some cases, academics, who are often the last people to admit their inadequacies, presume they can prepare distance learning materials without having had any training to do so or any personal experience of what it is like to study at a distance.

The increase in distance learning at postgraduate level has meant that students who are resident in a different location to their host university are making demands on university libraries in the area in which they live (see Unwin, Bolton and Stephens, 1995). Before the ending of the binary divide in 1992, there were reciprocal arrangements between universities and between polytechnics for undergraduates to use libraries in their vacations. Today, these arrangements are breaking down as a result of funding cuts and the expansion of student numbers, and, where they exist, they rarely extend to postgraduate students. Some course providers take the view that distance learning courses should include all the reading material which a student will need so as to minimize, or, in some cases, completely eradicate the need to visit a library. Others take the opposite view, believing that using libraries and developing information retrieval skills should form a central part of postgraduate study. Too often, however, it is the student, rather than the course provider, who has to establish whether they can gain access to a university library within reasonable travelling distance of their home or workplace. If an arrangement can be made, it will usually mean that the student has to pay a substantial fee to acquire external borrowing rights or they may be restricted to reading and browsing rights.

Lack of attention to these issues adds to the barriers which prevent teachers from gaining access to the literature on education and closes down opportunities for people to explore beyond the confines of the packaged materials selected by their tutors (see Unwin, 1994). New technologies may help course providers, librarians and students alike to overcome some of these problems but any solutions must be predicated on opening up access to intellectual resources rather than on a reductionist approach which puts cost before learning.

Distance learning can, of course, simply replicate the university-centred approaches and hierarchies referred to earlier in this chapter. To see distance learning merely as a marketing ploy in which traditional courses are repackaged, is, however, to miss a major educational opportunity. The final section of this chapter suggests the ways in which postgraduate courses run at a distance can be combined with collaborative on-site projects to support teachers in their work as researchers. This section is based on work I have been doing with two colleges located several miles from my own university.

Working together: college and university collaboration

To work effectively, it helps if relationships are based on honesty and trust. University education departments and colleges therefore, have to identify what it is they want from the collaboration, the nature of the roles each will play and the particular areas of expertise each can bring. There can be a shared agenda which, hopefully, will strengthen over time, but each stakeholder has to also recognize its distinct and discrete needs and goals. In addition, the individual practitioners who participate must be allowed to retain the level of individuality they would exercise if they were acting as a traditional student of a postgraduate course, that is if they had simply applied to the university in a private capacity. In order for this to happen, the academics must demonstrate their own professional integrity and not be seen as promoting the needs of one stakeholder above another.

It is in the need to protect the rights of the individual that the 'distance learning' factor can be used to important advantage. By linking the on-site activity to an academic course, the college has to release staff to attend residential events which allow staff to separate themselves physically and mentally from the workplace in order to gain new perspectives and meet colleagues from other institutions.

124

Since 1994, I have been working with two colleges who wanted to combine their interest in developing teachers as researchers with an opportunity for members of staff to gain a postgraduate qualification. The project has, so far, identified the following set of aims:

1   to introduce staff to the research process;
2   to enable staff to generate ideas for research projects which extend their practice and address questions which arise out of their practice;
3   to help staff understand the way in which their research interests relate to the wider post-16 context;
4   to introduce staff to other research being conducted in their areas of interest and to the range of relevant literature in the social sciences;
5   to give academic credit within a postgraduate degree programme for work produced as a result of action research projects;
6   to stimulate developments in the structure and content of the degree programme arising from issues raised by the collaborative activity;
7   to encourage joint research activity in which academics and practitioners work together.

The project is moving forward in the following stages: firstly, the university has led workshops with all teaching and support staff in the colleges to explore the ways in which research methodologies can be applied to small scale investigations; secondly, staff have been invited to submit ideas for research projects (working individually or in small teams) to a working group comprised of senior college staff and academics who then work with staff to determine the feasibility of the projects and allocate any necessary resources; thirdly, any staff who wish to participate in the postgraduate course linked to the programme can do so either by enrolling for the whole course or by selecting an appropriate module which will enable them to prepare their research project data in such a way as to meet the requirements for gaining academic credit; and, fourthly, the progress of and results from the projects are disseminated via staff led workshops.

Some staff in the two colleges expressed suspicion in the early stages of the collaboration. They questioned the motives of the university and of their college managements. The university, they argued, might be promoting collaboration simply as a means to increase student numbers or to gain research material which academics could then 'steal' and use it for their own publication purposes. As for the college managements, they might see action research as an opportunity to get staff to do even more work and to find excuses for introducing new ways of working which staff might normally resist. These issues, which challenge the perceptions, attitudes and hidden agendas of all the stakeholders, were discussed at length with small groups of staff at the beginning of the project and will be revisited as the project develops. The discussions have helped to clarify the role of the university which, so far, has taken on the following responsibilities:

1 support for nominated research supervisors within the colleges who act as mentors to staff;
2 chairing discussion groups to examine research methodologies and findings;
3 acting as a bridge between management and staff, between departments in the colleges, between the academic and vocational areas in the colleges, and between teaching and support staff.

There are many challenges to face if collaboration is to work to the benefit of all the stakeholders and those involved have to be prepared to be flexible in order to adapt and change their approach as the relationships cement.

Conclusion

Changes may be imposed from external bodies on the relationship between further and higher education with regard to the design, content and provision of professional development courses. Any changes which restrict the ability of education professionals to examine and critique their practice must be resisted but we have to demonstrate that the relationship between further and higher education is a dynamic one and can itself adapt to the changing environment.

The benefits of collaboration will depend on the nature of the relationship and some may develop and change over time. In general, though, the following might be held up as goals worth striving for:
1 to help keep alive and foster a critical exploration of education policy and practice;
2 to help education professionals critique their profession and put them in touch with research findings;
3 to help education professionals identify and celebrate effective practice, encourage change where necessary and introduce new ways of working;
4 to give education professionals a voice to be heard by the professional, policy making and academic communities;
5 to challenge the academic research community to share its work more widely;
6 to encourage academics to learn from practitioners;
7 to revitalize accredited professional development courses.

Bibliography

ACAS (1988), *Employee Appraisal* (Advisory Booklet No. 11), ACAS, England.

Adams, M. (1994), *Implementing Investors in People in Colleges*, The Adams Consultancy Ltd., Buckinghamshire.

Adams, M. (1995), *Staff Development Challenges and Opportunities*, LASER Advisory Council, London.

Argyris, C. and Schon, D. (1980), *Theory in Practice: Increasing Professional Effectiveness*, Jossey Bass, San Francisco.

Alexander, R. (1990), 'Partnership in Initial Teacher Training: Confronting the Issues' in Booth, M., Furlong, J., and Wilkin, M. (eds.) *Partnership in Initial Teacher Training*, Cassell, London.

Ashworth, P.(1992), 'Being competent and having competencies' in *Journal of Further and Higher Education*, vol.16, no.3.

Ashworth, P. and Saxton, J.(1990), 'On competence', *Journal of Further and Higher Educaion*, vol.14 no.1.

Audit Commission/OFSTED (1993), *Unfinished Business: full-time educational courses for 16-19 year olds*, HMSO, London.

Avis, J. (1993), 'Policy orientated research: the seduction of science and the teacher researcher', *Educational Review*, vol. 45 no. 3.

Ball, S.J. (1990), 'Management as Moral Technology' in Ball, S. J. (ed.), *Foucault and Education- Disciplines and Knowledge*, Routledge, London.

Bloom, B.S. (ed.) (1956), *Taxonomy of Educational Objectives*, Handbook 1, Cognitive Domain, Longman, London.

Bloor M. and Butterworth C. (1991), 'Accrediting prior learning on an in-service course for teachers' *Aspects of Educational Technology*, vol. XXIV, *Realising Human Potential*, Kogan Page, London.

Bloor M. and Butterworth, C. (1994), 'The professional development model of APL: some problems of validity and assessment', SCUTREA July Conference Proceedings.

Booth, M. (1993), 'The effectiveness and the role of the mentor in school: the students' view', *Cambridge Journal of Educaton*, vol. 23, no.2.

Boud, D., Keogh, R. and Walker, D. (1985), *Reflection: Turning Experience into Learning*, Kogan Page, London.

Bright, B.(ed.) (1989), *Theory and practice in the study of Adult Education: the epistemological debate*, Routledge, London.

Bull, A. (1985), 'The use of behavioural objectives', *Journal of Further and Higher Education*, vol.9, no.1.

Butt R.L.(1984), 'Arguments for using biography in understanding teacher thinking' in Halkes, R. and Olson, J.K. (eds.) *Teacher Thinking*, Swets and Zeitlinger, Lisse.

Butterworth, C. and Edwards, R. (1993), 'Accrediting prior learning at a distance', *Open Learning*, vol. 8 no.13, November.

Calderhead,J. and James, C. (1992), 'Recording student teachers' learning experiences', *Journal of Further and Higher Education*, vol. 16 no. 1.

Callendar, C.(1992), 'Will NVQ's work?' *IMS Report* No.228, Institute of Manpower Studies, University of Sussex, Brighton.

Carr, W. and Kemis, S. (1986), *Becoming Critical*, The Falmer Press, London.

Chambers, P. (1992), *The Future of Cert Ed/PGCE in FE*, unpublished conference address to SCETT conference on FE Teacher Education and Training, 6/2/92.

Charnley, A.H. and Jones, H.A. (1979), *The Concept of Success in Adult Literacy*, ALBSU, London.

Chown, A. (1994), 'Beyond competence?', *British Journal of In-service Education*, vol.20, no.2.

Chown, A. and Last, J. (1993), 'Can the NCVQ model be used for teacher training?' *Journal of Further and Higher Education*, vol. 17, no.2.

Clark, P. (1995), 'Core skills for competitiveness - a CBI perspective', *Literacy Today*, no. 2, March, National Literacy Trust, London.

Combs, A.W. and Soper, D.W. (1963), 'Perceptual organisation of effective counsellors', *Journal of Counselling Psychology*, vol. 10 no.3.

Department of Education and Science (DES) (1984), Circular 3/84, *Initial Teacher Training: Approval of Courses*, HMSO, London.

Department of Education and Science et al. (DES) (1991), *Education and Training for the 21st Century* (2 volumes), HMSO, London.

Department of Education and Science (DES) (1992), Circular 9/92, *Initial Teacher Training (Secondary Phase)*, HMSO, London.

Ecclestone, K. (1993), 'Competence: the implications for education and training', *Competence: The 1993 Report*, AVCET, London.

Ecclestone, K. (1995) 'Look before we leap at NVQs', *Times Educational Supplement*, TES2 Section, 6/1/95, London.

Education Act (1993), HMSO, London.

Edwards, J. and Giles, H. (1984), 'Applications of the Social Psychology of Language: Sociolinguistics and Education', in Trudgill, P.(ed.), *Applied Sociolinguistics*, Academic Press, London.

Edwards, R, and Usher, R. (1995), 'Confessing all? A postmodern guide to the guidance and counselling of adults' in *Studies in the Education of Adults*, vol. 27, no. 1.

Elbaz, F. (1990), 'Knowledge and discourse: the evolution of research of teacher thinking' in Day, C., Pope, M., and Denicolo, P. (eds.) *Insight into Teachers' Thinking and Practice*, The Falmer Press, London.

Elliott, J. and Sarland, C. (1995), 'A study of "teachers as researchers" in the context of award-bearing courses and research degrees', *British Educational Research Journal*, vol. 21, no. 3.

Eraut, M. (1994), *Developing Professional Knowledge and Competence*, The Falmer Press London.

Furlong, J.(1990), 'School Based Training: The Students' Views' in Booth, M., Furlong, J., and Wilkin, M. (eds.), *Partnership in Initial Teacher Training*, Cassell, London.

Further and Higher Education Act (1992), HMSO, London.

Further Education Funding Council (1992) a, *Funding Learning*, FEFC, Coventry.

Further Education Funding Council (1992) b, *College Strategic Plans*, Circular 92/18, FEFC, Coventry.

Further Education Funding Council (1993), *Assessing Achievement*, Circular 93/28, FEFC, Coventry.

Further Education Funding Council (1994) a, *Guidance on the Recurrent Funding Methodology 1994/95*, FEFC, Coventry.

Further Education Funding Council (FEFC) (1994) b, *Quality and Standards in Further Education in England*, FEFC, Coventry.

Further Education Funding Council (1994) c, *Measuring Achievement*, Circular 94/31, FEFC, Coventry.

Further Education Unit (1981), *Transition and Access: A Review of Further and Higher Education in London*, ILEA, London.

Further Education Unit (1984), *Towards a Competence-based System*, FEU, London.

Further Education Unit (1988), *NCVQ and its Implications*, FEU, London.

Further Education Unit (1989), *FE Staff Development Networks*, FEU, London.

Further Education Unit (1992), *TDLB Standards in F.E.*, FEU, london.

Further Education Unit (1994), *Examining Assessment*, FEU, London.

Further Education Unit (1995), *Newsletter*, Spring, FEU, London.

Gee, R. (1994), John Baillie Memorial Lecture, NATFHE, London.

Gee, R. (1995), 'AfC rejects narrow competence testing', *FE News*, No.14, February.

Gibbs, G. (1988), *Learning by doing*, FEU, London.

Gonczi, A. (1994), 'Competency based assessment in the professions in Australia', *Assessment in Education*, vol. 1 no.1.

Handy, C. (1990), *The Age of Unreason*, Arrow Books, London.

Haycocks, N. (1975), *The Training of Teachers for Further Education*: report by the Sub-Committee on the Training of Teachers for Further Education relating to the training of full-time teachers in further education, HMSO, London.

Her Majesty's Inspectorate (1992), *Training for Teaching in Further and Adult Education*, No.19/91/NS, HMSO, London.

Hodge, B. (ed.), (1981), *Communication and the Teacher*, Longman, London.

Hodkinson, P. (1992), 'Alternative models of competence in vocational education and training', *Journal of Further and Higher Education*, vol.16 no.2.

Hodkinson, P. and Issit, M. (eds.) (1995), *The Challenge of Competence*, Cassell Education, London.

Honey, P. and Mumford, A. (1982), *The Manual of Learning Styles*, P. Honey, Maidenhead.

Hyland, T. (1993), 'Professionalism, competence and education for training', *Competence: The 1993 Report*, AVCET, London.

Hyland, T. (1994), 'Professionalism and competence in post-school education', Paper delivered at SCETT Conference entitled 'An Overview of Post 16 Training', London.

Jarvis, P. (1994), 'Learning practical knowledge', *Journal of Further and Higher Education*, vol. 18 no. 1.

Jessup, G. (1991), *Outcomes: NVQ's and the Emerging Model of Education and Training*, The Falmer Press, London.

Julka, L. (1995), 'Language, culture and GNVQ assessment' *Focus and Care Standard*, vol. 2 Issue 6.

Kelchtermans, G. and Vandenberghe, R. (1994), 'Teachers' professional development: a biographical perspective', *Journal of Curriculum Studies*, vol. 26, no.1.

Kelly, A.V. (1993), 'Education as a field of study', *Journal of Education for Teaching: international research and pedagogy*, vol. 19, no. 2.

Kolb, D. and Fry R. (1975), 'Towards an applied theory of learning' in Cooper, C. (ed.), *Theories of Group Processes*, John Wiley, London.

Kolb, D.(1984), *Experiential Learning: experience as a source of learning and development*, Prentice-Hall, Englewood-Cliffs NJ.

Lankshear C. with Lawlor M. (1987), *Literacy Schooling and Revolution*, Falmer Press, East Sussex.

McCann, I. and Radford, R. (1990), 'Mentoring for Teachers: The Collaborative Approach' in Caldwell, B.J. and Carter, E.M.A. (eds.), *The Return of the Mentor*, The Falmer Press, London.

MacDonald R.M.(1973), 'Behavioural objectives: a critical review', *Instructional Science 2*.

Marshall, K. (1991), 'NVQs: An assessment of the 'outcomes' approach to education and training', *Journal of Further and Higher Education*, vol.15, no.3.

McIntyre, D., (1990), 'The Oxford Internship Scheme and the Cambridge Analytical Framework: Models of Partnership in Initial Teacher Education' in Booth M., Furlong, J., and Wilkin, M. (eds.), *Partnership in Initial Teacher Training*, Cassell, London.

McIntyre, D. and Haggar, H. (1993), 'Teachers' Expertise and Models of Mentoring' in McIntyre, D., Haggar, H. and Wilkin, M. (eds.), *Mentoring Perspectives on School Based Education*, Kogan Page, London.

Miller, N. and Morgan, D. (1993), 'Called to account: the CV as an autobiographical practice', *Sociology*, vol. 27, no. 1 February.

NATFHE (1991), *Guidelines for Negotiating Appraisal Schemes in the Maintained Education Sector*, London.

National Council for Vocational Qualifications (NCVQ) (1995), *NVQ Criteria and Guidance*, Department of Employment, London.

Norris, N. (1991), 'The trouble with competence', *Cambridge Journal of Education*, vol. 21 no. 3.

Northern Region Staff Development Network (1983), *Small Scale and Homespun: the case of the Northern Region Staff Development Network*, Newcastle Polytechnic, Newcastle Upon Tyne.

Pedlar, M., Boydell, T. and Burgoyne, J. (1989), 'Towards the learning company', *Management Education and Development*, vol. 20 no. 1.

Peters, T.J. and Waterman, R.H. (1982), *In Search of Excellence*, Harper and Row, New York

Raggatt, P. (1994), 'Implementing NVQs in colleges' *Journal of Further and Higher Education*, vol. 18 no.1.

Ramsay, J. (1993), 'The hybrid course: competence and behaviourism in higher education' *Journal of Further and Higher Education*, vol. 17, no.3.

Ryle, G. (1949), *The Concept of Mind*, Penguin, London.

Schon, D. (1987), *Educating the Reflective Practitioner*, Jossey Bass, San Francisco.

Schon D. (1991), *The Reflective Practitioner: how professionals think in action*, Avebury, Aldershot.

Smithers, A. (1994), Interview, *Furthering Education*, Winter 1994.

Smithers, A. (1995) 'Able to dribble but not to score?', *Times Educational Supplement*, 10/2/95.

Somekh, B. (1995), 'Action research and improvement in social endeavours', *British Educational Research Journal*, vol. 21 no. 3.

Stark, S. and McAleavy G. (1992), 'Initiating a competence-based teacher training programme in FE', *Journal of Further and Higher Education*, vol. 16 no. 2.

131

Tickle, L. (1993), 'The wish of Odysseus? New teachers' receptiveness to mentoring', in McIntyre, D., Haggar, H. and Wilkin, M (eds.), *Mentoring Perspectives on School Based Education*, Kogan Page, London.

Times Educational Supplement (TES) (1993), 'Either compete, co-operate or die', 26/3/93.

Times Higher Educational Supplement (THES) (1993), 'FE Heads go radical on funding', 7/5/93.

Times Higher Educational Supplement (THES) (1994) a, 'Dropouts skew FE targets', 14/1/94.

Times Higher Educational Supplement (THES) (1994) b, 'Curate's egg found in colleges', 28/1/94.

Tuxworth, E. (1982), *Competency in Teaching*, Further Education Unit, London.

Tuxworth, E. (1989), 'Competence-based Education and Training: Background and Origins', in Burke, J. W. (ed.) *Competency-based Education and Training*, The Falmer Press, Sussex.

UDACE (1989), *Understanding competence: a development paper*, NIACE, Leicester.

Unwin, L. (1991), 'Enabling learning: raising the profile of staff development' in McNay, I. (ed.) *Visions of Post Compulsory Education*, SRHE/Open University, Buckingham.

Unwin, L.(1994), I'm a real student now', *Journal of Further and Higher Education*, vol. 18, no.1.

Unwin, L., Bolton, N. and Stephens, K. (1995), 'The role of the library in distance learning', *Library and Information Briefings*, Number 60.

Ware, J. (1993), *A Study of English Workshop Provision*, unpublished MPhil thesis, submitted to University of Greenwich.

Wharfe, L. and Burrows, A. (1990), 'Partnership: A CNAA Perspective' in Booth, M., Furlong, J., and Wilkin, M.(eds.), *Partnership in Initial Teacher Training*, Cassell, London.

Wilkin, M. (1990), 'The Development of Partnership in the United Kingdom' in Booth M., Furlong, J., and Wilkin, M., (eds.) *Partnership in Initial Teacher Training*, Cassell, London.

Williams, Anne (1993), 'Teacher perceptions of their needs as mentors in the context of developing school based initial teacher education', *British Education Research Journal*, vol.19, no.4.

Winter, R. (1992), 'Quality management or the educative workplace: alternative versions of competence-based education', *Journal of Further and Higher Education*, vol. 16 no. 3.

Wolf, A. (1993), 'Assessment issues and problems in a criterion- based system', Further Education Unit, London.

Wragg, T. (1990), 'The Two Routes into Teaching' in Booth, M., Furlong, J., and Wilkin, M. (eds.), *Partnership in Initial Teacher Training*, Cassell, London.

Young, M., Lucas ,N., Sharp, G., and Cunningham B., (1995), *Teacher Education for the Further Education Sector: Training the Lecturers of the Future*, Institute of Education University of London, London.

Index

evaluation 4, 11, 19, 28, 42, 44, 46
  47, 51, 55, 77, 79, 81, 82, 83, 85,
  88, 90, 97, 101, 102, 108-109,
  110, 113, 114, 115
experiential learning 27, 46, 48, 49-
  50, 51, 55

feedback 37, 38, 39, 40, 41, 51, 52,
  54, 55, 79, 83, 94, 110, 113
FEFC
  funding criteria/methodology 1-2,
  9, 33, 61, 76, 99-100, 117
  inspections 2-3, 5, 9, 42, 90, 91,
  93, 96
  reports 3, 5, 9, 42, 99, 101-105,
  111, 112-113
flexible learning 5, 23, 60-72, 117,
  123

human resource management 3, 78-
  79, 82, 83, 90, 92, 96, 97, 98

incorporation 2, 3, 5, 9, 13, 20, 61,
  73, 76, 78-83, 87, 95, 121, 123
induction 11-12, 13, 61, 77, 78, 96
industry lead bodies 23, 28, 121
Investors in People 5, 28, 87-98, 103,
  104, 106, 107,110, 111, 112, 113

learning agenda 17, 63, 64, 67, 69
  organisation 122
  style 48, 55
  support 60, 61
  theory 18, 44, 49
libraries 123-124

management team 74, 95, 96, 97
  training 4, 78, 104
marketing 10, 77, 83, 115, 124
mentoring 4, 13, 14-15, 33-43
mission/mission statement 73, 74,
  75, 78
modular curriculum 24, 47

monitoring 11, 14-16, 36, 40, 81,
  83, 101, 108-110, 114, 115

national standard 23, 24, 28, 31, 87,
  88, 89, 90, 93, 98
negotiation 21, 24, 41, 68, 99, 100,
  108
networks/consortia 5, 69, 71, 84-85
National Vocational Qualifications
  24, 26, 27, 28, 32, 61, 69, 71, 75,
  83, 104

occupational mapping 31
open learning 60, 69, 123

part-time staff 75, 99, 102, 103-105,
  110-111, 115, 116
partnership 4, 7-19, 33, 34
peer support 10, 16, 17, 19, 42, 54
portfolio 5, 44-59, 93-94, 97
professional development 4, 5, 6, 18,
  24, 31, 42, 44-48, 50, 55, 56-59,
  76, 78, 79, 80, 92, 97, 98, 100,
  103, 109, 114, 116, 117, 119, 121,
  126
  national framework for 19, 24, 116
profiles 25, 26, 27, 31
progression 21, 23, 24, 61, 67, 72
Project 2000 48
promotion 42, 100, 105

quality assurance 2-3, 13, 15, 19, 21,
  42, 73, 78, 79, 81, 83, 94, 106,
  112-113, 115
  development 25, 28, 58, 70, 73,
  87, 89-92, 98, 114
  systems 5, 79, 83, 87-98

research 6, 117-125
reflective practice 21, 26, 29, 31, 41,
  46, 47, 48, 49-50, 51, 53-54, 55,
  57, 58
resource-based learning 5, 23, 60, 69

135